ENC

Effective prayer is a non-negotiable to the Christian life—I emphasize the word *effective*. The problem is many believers have settled for a form of prayer that becomes religious, stale, and downright boring. It was the late general Dr. C. Peter Wagner who provoked the body of Christ to engage a form of prayer that produced measurable results.

Christy Johnston (along with her amazing husband Nate) have become friends and great encouragers to me (and, I know, to many other leaders in the body of Christ). I have specifically witnessed the Lord raise up a new breed of intercessory "watchman," and Christy is truly one of these prayer leaders for a new generation. Christy is not a prayer theorist; she is a practitioner who regularly sees and leads others into results.

Releasing Prophetic Solutions will upgrade your prayer life, showing you how to download supernatural solutions from heaven, boldly pray them, and see measurable results through your prayers.

—Larry Sparks, MDiv.
Publisher, Destiny Image

An incredible communicator and highly trained intercessor, Christy Johnston is a voice for the generations. In *Releasing Prophetic Solutions*, Christy takes her reader through an intense and yet practical training to partner with the Father's heart in prayer in such a way that homes, families, and nations are changed. Christy is uniquely positioned to share this message as a woman who has not only lived out the strategies she shares in this book, but as someone who can translate intense spiritual truths into practical everyday solutions. Christy can be trusted, her message needs to be heard, and the kingdom of God will advance when prophetic prayer is released into the world.

—Becky Thompson
Author of *Hope Unfolding*

Christy Johnston's book *Releasing Prophetic Solutions* is a must-read for anyone who truly needs a fresh wind of God's Spirit in their life. This book will stir up the gifting of life-changing, atmospher-shifting, prophetic prayer and intercession! The revelation that is released will jump off the page and remind your spirit who you are and what is available to you through prophetic prayer. Christy walks in this anointing in her everyday life, and I have seen firsthand how she moves through her day as a wife and mother and simultaneously blesses everyone around her with sharp, accurate words from heaven. The fresh word in this book and revelation will open your heart wide and allow the Spirit of God to come *in and move.*

—Cammy Brickell
Actress, speaker, comedian

There are books that teach on prophetic prayer, but then there are life-changing books that are a catalyst into deeper dimensions of prophetic prayer. *Releasing Prophetic Solutions* is simply that. An absolute must-have in your spiritual arsenal. I've had the honor of walking with and learning from Christy Johnston for quite some time now. God has masterfully graced Christy not only to expound biblically on how to navigate in prophetic intercession, but within each page from front to back she takes every reader into authentic encounters from her personal journeys and remarkable history with God. I encourage you to not only take the valued principles housed in every chapter but to share this amazing new book with family, friends, churches, and small groups. Get ready to go on an adventurous dive into the river of revelation with God today. God wants to mark you as a prophetic solutionist in the earth to release His glory. *Releasing Prophetic Solutions* is a real game changer. Read it today; trust me, you won't be disappointed.

—Torrey Marcel Harper
Senior Leader, Global Prayer Room, NYC
Habitation Church

This book carries a catalytic message of the power of prayer and the arsenal of heaven that is accessible to every believer. Your faith will be ignited and taken into new atmospheres of possibility as your vision begins to be empowered with solutions that will unlock transformation in the earth.

—Fiorella Giordano
8th Ocean

You can tell when someone is marked by a mandate from heaven. Christy Johnston is one whose heart is branded by fire and whose voice carries heaven's thunder. We have journeyed with Christy and Nate Johnston for many years now and their passion for justice, prophetic purity, and breakthrough has not only marked our lives but awakened a movement of new-breed, fearless, and unrelenting "ground strikers"!

Releasing Prophetic Solutions will mark you with this same spirit and give you practical keys for redemptive solutions in your life.

What I love most about this book though is that Christy truly lives it. She is a fierce warrior who partners activism with anointed grace. We love Christy and Nate, and we are honored to not just recommend these pages to you but commend our friends to you as those who walk with authenticity and uncommon zeal. Christy and Nate are not intimidated by giants, and as you read this neither will you be!

—Ben and Jodie Hughes
Pour It Out Ministries
www.pouritout.org
Authors of *When God Breaks In* and *The King's Decree*

Finally, a book that splendidly teaches *you* about the wonderful partnership between you and Abba (Daddy) Father. Skillfully with both story and Scriptures, Christy Johnston makes a most easy-to-grasp case that no matter what your personality or even your past mistakes, you are called and qualified *right now* to jointly know God's will for your life (and often others) and you are *now* qualified to put into practice the stories and lessons within the pages of this amazing book. The time for excuses is over as you quickly understand that nothing else is stopping your success with a relationship and partnership with God the Father, Jesus His Son, and the Holy Spirit. Get this book and while you're at it, I'd buy one for a friend too. It's that good!

—Steve Shultz, Founder
THE ELIJAH LIST
ELIJAHStreams TV Program

RELEASING PROPHETIC SOLUTIONS

CHRISTY JOHNSTON

RELEASING PROPHETIC SOLUTIONS

PRAYING HEAVEN'S PROMISES OVER
YOUR HOME, FAMILY, AND NATION

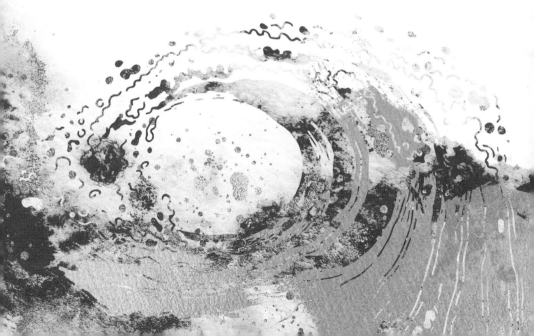

DESTINY IMAGE® PUBLISHERS, INC.
P.O. Box 310, Shippensburg, PA 17257-0310
"Promoting Inspired Lives."

This book and all other Destiny Image and Destiny Image Fiction books are available at Christian bookstores and distributors worldwide.

Cover design by Eileen Rockwell

For more information on foreign distributors, call 717-532-3040.

Reach us on the Internet: www.destinyimage.com.

ISBN 13 TP: 978-0-7684-5345-4

ISBN 13 eBook: 978-0-7684-5346-1

ISBN 13 HC: 978-0-7684-5348-5

ISBN 13 LP: 978-0-7684-5347-8

For Worldwide Distribution, Printed in the U.S.A.

1 2 3 4 5 6 7 8 / 24 23 22 21 20

DEDICATION

I DEDICATE THIS BOOK TO MY FAMILY:

My husband, Nate, for every step you have walked alongside me through this process, both in the discovery of prophetic prayer and in the birthing of this book. Thank you for being my greatest cheerleader and best friend.

To my children, Charlotte and Sophie—may you always walk in the footsteps of Jesus, in knowing His voice and releasing it into the earth.

I pray you will run further than I ever have or will.

To my parents, Terry and Suzy, thank you for teaching me resilient and bold faith. Thank you for modeling to me as a child how to see with my eyes of faith and to call into alignment those things that are not as though they are.

I love you all.

ACKNOWLEDGEMENTS

Larry Sparks—Thank you for releasing the prophetic word over me that set the wheels of this book into motion and gave me the language to understand how to release the message.

Tina Pugh—I am beyond thankful for your endless patience in this process of writing my first book. You have been the most wonderful help a writer could ask for.

Wendy McKaskill—You may not realize it, but your faithfulness to pursue the heart of God and His voice has affected my life in more ways than you could ever know. Thank you for modeling a life of prayer.

"It is abnormal for a Christian not to have an appetite for the impossible. It has been written into our spiritual DNA to hunger for the impossibilities around us to bow at the name of Jesus."

—Bill Johnson, *When Heaven Invades Earth: A Practical Guide to a Life of Miracles*

CONTENTS

FOREWORD

Scripture tells us that the testimony of Jesus is the spirit of prophecy (see Rev. 19:10). A study of the life of Jesus as He walked the earth reveals that Jesus is the Answer! He was the answer to everyone who came to Him, whether they had run out of wine at a wedding or needed a loved one healed or raised from the dead. Jesus manifested Himself as the answer to everyone who came to Him with a problem.

In the same way, we as His body, the temple of His Holy Spirit, are called to manifest Jesus. The very heart and purpose of prophecy is to reveal the testimony of Jesus, the answer in every situation. In this book, Christy shares the importance, as well as the practical how-tos, of prophetically releasing solutions to a world that desperately needs them.

Prophetic words are, however, not inevitabilities but invitations requiring our response. According to First Timothy 1:18, believers are exhorted to wage warfare with prophecies. Christy is well acquainted with prophetic warfare prayer and teaches us from the Word of God and through genuine breakthroughs she has seen in prayer to wage a "good warfare," so that the will of God can be done on earth as it is in heaven. The partnership between intercession and prophecy is an essential key to understand as we, the body of Christ, step into our rightful role as kings and priests in the earth.

In my years of mentoring and training prophetic people, one thing I have found is that prophetic people are sensitive! And sensitive people can easily take on the burdens of the world. Without proper understanding, prophets and intercessors can find themselves weighed down with burdens. We are called to cast our cares on the Lord (Ps. 55:22), to be anxious for nothing, but in everything, with prayer and supplication, with thanksgiving, make our requests known to God (Phil. 4:6). And the promise is that God's peace will guard our hearts and minds. God wants His people to live in "righteousness, peace and joy" (Rom. 14:17), and the keys Christy shares really are solutions for those who are given to carrying and feeling the burdens of others. As intense and necessary as intercessory prophetic prayer is, it can and should be an easy burden and a light yoke.

Christy is a true prophetic warrior and a lover of God who understands the great power of partnering prophecy and prayer. I am grateful for the blessing this book is to the body of Christ as we step into the fullness of all we are called to be.

—Katherine Ruonala
Senior Leader, Glory City Church
Brisbane, Australia
Author of *Living in the Miraculous*, *Wilderness to Wonders*,
Life with the Holy Spirit, and
Speak Life: Creating Your World with Your Words

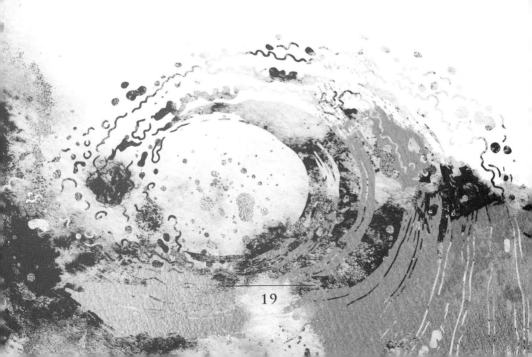

PART ONE

PROPHETIC PRAYER

CHAPTER ONE

WHAT IS PROPHETIC PRAYER?

"We tend to use prayer as a last resort, but God wants it to be our first line of defence. We pray when there's nothing else we can do, but God wants us to pray before we do anything at all." —Oswald Chambers

We know prayer is powerful, but what happens when a son or a daughter partners their authority in prayer with the potency of prophecy? Could Acts 2:17 be pointing to something that we are moving into the complete fulfillment of? Where it says, *"This is what I will do in the last days—I will pour out my Spirit on everybody and cause your sons and daughters to prophesy, and your young men will see visions, and your old men will experience dreams from God"* (Acts 2:17), the Greek word used in this verse for "pour out" is *ekcheo* (Strong's, G1632). It is the same word that is used throughout the New Testament in reference to the Blood of the Lamb and the pouring forth of the Holy Spirit. It speaks of spilling, running out, gushing out, and covering completely. It paints the picture for you and me that the days in which we are alive are to be covered in the Spirit of the Lord. Our mouths are to be gushing forth His words. Could the world we currently see, with all of its problems, be transformed through the creative power of God's spoken words pouring forth through the mouths of His sons and daughters? I wholeheartedly believe so. Many believe that the miracle-working God of the Bible is not for today. This is a crafty lie of the enemy because he knows what has been prophesied about this time in which we live, and he will do anything to convince us into disempowerment. Our God, Jesus, is the same, yesterday, today, and forever (see Heb. 13:8). If what He spoke through the prophet Isaiah was the same for those who were alive then, I believe we need to wholeheartedly seize it for the time in which we are alive today.

> *Who has ever seen or heard of such a wonder? Could a country be born in a day? Can a nation be birthed so suddenly? Yet no sooner does Zion go into labor than she gives birth to sons! Yahweh, your God, says, "Do I allow you to conceive and not to give birth? Do I shut the womb when I'm the one who delivers?"* (Isaiah 66:8-9)

We have seen this prophecy fulfilled in part, when Israel was reborn in a day in 1948, but I believe we have not seen anything yet. God is the one who delivers, and I believe He is looking for a people in this hour who will partner their faith with Him through the power of their prophetic prayer and declarations and release the solutions of heaven into the earth. He is looking for a people who will prophesy His heart and cause that which is out of order to be realigned back into His original and intended design. What could that possibly look like? Heaven on earth, just as Jesus said: *"Manifest your kingdom realm, and cause your every purpose to be fulfilled on earth, just as it is fulfilled in heaven"* (Matt. 6:10). Pause on that for a moment. His *every purpose to be fulfilled on earth*, just as it is fulfilled in heaven. This is not wishful thinking; it is a firm promise of what can and will be attained, and I for one intend to be among those who says, "Yes, Father, may it be done through my life!"

When Jesus spoke these words, He was teaching His disciples a new way of praying. It is the power of prophetic prayer to speak the answers of God's kingdom realm into the existence of the natural realm. My hope and prayer for you is that as you read the coming pages of this book, the fires of your heart will be stoked with the passion to see this promise fulfilled through your own life as well. Does this mean that the earth will discontinue to have its problems? Obviously not. As long as we live on this earth, we will have the enemy working against us, but that does not mean that we are to have a victim mentality where we raise a white flag in defeat and say, "Let's just wait until heaven."

YOU HAVE THE BALL

The word for prophecy used in Acts 2:17 is the Greek word *propheteuo* (Strong's, G4395), and it means to speak under divine inspiration to foretell events (fortune-tellers are mere counterfeits of true prophecy) and exercise the prophetic office. This tells me that even those who are not gifted with the prophetic office can still exercise the prophetic voice of God. It also tells me that we should be moving in an offensive prayer lifestyle. Not the kind that reacts to the problems of the world, but foresees them ahead of time and speaks the solutions of God's heart, effectively dismantling and disempowering the enemy right in the middle of his plans—before they materialize. I for one am absolutely done with the reactionary, #prayforthiscity hashtags that circulate on social media following a tragedy. Please don't misunderstand me—I value and treasure prayer; especially in the wake of a tragedy, it is a needed aspect of healing. What I am saying is, I want to see God's people moving so effectively in offensive prayer that we divert many of the tragedies to begin with, if not all. Where our eyes and ears are so in tune with the heart of God that by the divine inspiration of His Spirit we are able to see an attack before it eventuates. When we see it, we dismantle it before it can manifest. Could the realization of the Father's every purpose fulfilled in the earth be that with one hand we are rebuilding that which has been stolen in the past, and with the other hand frustrating every plan of the enemy? Rather than satan's plans frustrating us, I believe it is time we fully frustrate his. Could we see the end of shootings across America? Could we see the manifestation of natural storms dissipate in their infancy to His spoken name? Could we truly see His Spirit poured out and nations reborn in a day? If we are to take Him at His word, then the answer is a resounding *yes*. God has promised men and women, young and old, dreams and visions—could these prophetic dreams and visions hold the answers of His Spirit to release His kingdom into the earth? I believe so. Then it is time we begin to activate what He is speaking and release His solutions into the earth.

In one of my favorite books on the topic of prayer, *The Happy Intercessor*, Beni Johnson writes:

On a football team you have a defensive team and an offensive team. The defensive team tries to steal the football from the opposing offensive team. The defensive team will try to figure out the offensive team's strategies and plays. The offensive team, however, has the advantage in that they have the ball. With their skill and different plays, they proceed to carry the football down the field to make a touchdown. The offensive team calls the plays, for they have the ball.

...For intercessors, it is extremely important to understand that God has already given us the ball. We are the offensive team. If you don't understand that, if you are not praying from a place of victory, then you will be an intercessor whose prayer life is marked with defeat. You will be one who is always trying to protect what God has given you from the devil's plans or, worse yet, running after the devil and trying to figure out what he is doing. How wrong is that? If you do not understand that God has already given you the ball, you will live in fear and pray from a place of lack.[1]

First, let me just say for anyone who may be wondering if you have picked up a book about intercession when you may not consider yourself an intercessor—I have written this for every believer. I believe that just like prophecy, while some are called to the office of a prophet and others are called to the office of intercession, we are *all* called to release prophecy and prayer. While you will see the mention of intercession a lot, my hopes and desire are to make it applicable to the person who doesn't believe they can pray with effectivity. When

I first read Beni's book many years ago, I felt much the same way. I used to think that an intercessor was someone who needed to spend five hours a day locked away in their wardrobe praying in tongues. As an early twenty-something-year-old, that did not sound very enticing—but as I read Beni's words, I realized how easy, effective, and even fun and adventurous prayer can be.

My hope is that this book will do the same for you—whether you are called to the office of a prophet or intercessor or not. God has called each of us to be transformers of the world around us, and it is done through the power of our spoken decrees. I remember mulling over those words in her book, "praying from a place of victory," and thinking to myself, *That's the game-changer.* What does it mean to pray from a place of victory? It means we see from a higher perspective. We have the ball, the authority of Christ, and therefore we aren't living in reaction to what the enemy is doing. We aren't chasing him down the field to try and get our authority back; we have it, and therefore what happens on the field is up to us to take it down to the other end and score. We are to frustrate his plans, not the other way around.

What could our lives, our families, and our nations look like if we truly believed and operated in this kingdom way of thinking? What kind of solutions could be produced through the effective and supernatural power of prophetic prayer? As David wrote in the Psalms:

> *With his breath he scatters the schemes of nations who oppose him; they will never succeed. His destiny-plan for the earth stands sure. His forever-plan remains in place and will never fail. Blessed and prosperous is that nation*

who has God as their Lord! They will be the people he has chosen for his own (Psalm 33:10-12).

Job reaffirms these words, where it is written, *"He thwarts the plans of the crafty, so that their hands achieve no success"* (Job 5:12 NIV). God desires to scatter the schemes of the crafty through you. His destiny-plan for the earth stands sure. What is that plan? That the earth would look like heaven. We have this purpose; to fulfill this mandate. To release the victorious answers of heaven into the earth. As we do, our spoken words will echo through into the doors of eternity. Your words carry the supernatural and creative power of God to move into the natural and overturn the impossibilities of this realm. The fact that Acts 2:17 tells us that His Spirit will be poured out on all flesh tells me that no one is excluded from this call. Men and women, young and old, we have all been given this commission to release the solutions of heaven into the earth.

My heart has been recently stirred and moved by the faith of the Roman officer (centurion) in Matthew 8. We all know the story— how the centurion approached Jesus asking Him for a miracle. When Jesus responded that He would go with him to the centurion's house, the officer replied:

> *Lord, who am I to have you come into my house? I under-stand your authority, for I too am a man who walks under authority and have authority over soldiers who serve under me. I can tell one to go and he'll go, and another to come and he'll come. I order my servants and they'll do whatever I ask. So I know that all you need to do is to stand here*

and command healing over my son and he will be instantly healed (Matthew 8:8-9).

The following verse tells us that Jesus was astonished when he heard this and remarked, *"He has greater faith than anyone I've encountered in Israel!"* (Matt. 8:10). The Bible then tells us that Jesus told the Roman officer to go home, because all that he believed for was done for him. This is, yet again, another insight into prophetic prayer. The Roman officer understood that his decrees were met with answers. He understood the authority of Jesus—that by a decree the solution was released. This is how prophetic prayer works. We speak the answer upon His authority, and a summons is released in heaven to usher in the answer.

SPEAKING THE ANSWER

I discovered the potency of combined prayer and prophecy much by accident. I did not fully realize in my moments of learning that I was partnering prayer with prophecy, but the results of these colliding forces have been monumental. The experiences I have walked through were like intentional ambushes of "purposeful training" set up by the Holy Spirit Himself. I should probably warn you that by picking up this book, you have essentially signed yourself up for these "not-so-accidental ambushes of training" from the Holy Spirit, so you might want to prepare yourself. You may still be asking, "What is the difference between prayer standing alone and prayer that is partnered with prophecy?" I see it this way: Prayer covers and surrounds situations; prayer petitions the Father and converses with

Him in intimate relationship. Prayer is a conversation between a son or a daughter and their Father. Prayer asks for answers. Prophecy is the intention of the Lord upon a matter; it is the answer of the Father's heart spoken into a problem ahead of time. When prayer is combined with prophecy, these types of conversations produce solutions. The strategies of the Father's heart that align with His Word are given and then spoken as a decree into the very core of a situation. This combination sets off a supernatural chain of events directly affecting the natural world and overturning impossibilities. When this prophetic solution is released from your mouth, while simultaneously offered up in prayer to the Father, it is so overpowering to the enemy that it not only destroys his current plans, it dismantles any of his future plans.

I have seen the strength of prophetic prayer at work in my own life. The more I have studied it, the more I have realized that it is not a gift for the intercessor alone, nor is it a gift for the prophet alone. I believe that prophetic prayer is a gift that is given to the entire body of Christ. I believe that every son and daughter has been given this supernatural weapon that has the cataclysmic ability to completely turn the tide of every battle that we face, whether it is a cultural battle, a battle within the home, or a battle of nations. Prophetic prayer moves in a similar way to John the Baptist who prepared the way of the Lord. Prophetic prayer strikes the ground of a situation like lightning, announcing and preparing the way for the Lord to come in with answers, overturning demonic strongholds with one touch of His might and power. This partnership abruptly interjects and halts the plans of the enemy with the intentions of God's heart. Prophetic prayer overturns that which was planned for evil, oftentimes before it even has a chance to manifest. When a son or daughter is moved by the intentions of their Father, they have the authority to pray from a vantage point that is devastating to the works of darkness.

Prophetic prayer is a partnership of force that is activated by your spoken word, authorizing the armies of heaven to respond on your behalf. Prophetic prayer emits aroma to the earth much like the fresh scents of spring that tell of warmer days on the horizon; it releases a heavenly fragrance into the earth that sings "change is in the air." Mountains that gloat pridefully of their apparent impossibility to defeat begin to crumble and disintegrate like dust the moment you speak with your authority. The sounds of your decrees are carried upon the winds of the Holy Spirit, who causes your words to fill atmospheres once dominated by darkness. Victory is emitted through the prophetic prayers of your voice. In his book *Authority in Prayer*, Dutch Sheets writes, "God has given you jurisdiction over your world—under His authority, of course. He wants you, not sin, demonic powers, negative circumstances, or any other outside force to govern it."[2] My prayer is that the fruit of this book would be the realization in your spirit of the authority in Christ that you carry, and as a result you would begin to release this authority upon the jurisdiction of your life, your family, and your nation and govern the earth with the solutions of heaven.

PROPHETIC PRAYER IN TRAINING

One of my first "training" sessions in releasing the prophetic solutions of God was not quite what you would expect. It was a time when an airline lost my suitcase. While a mere suitcase may seem irrelevant to the weightier issues of the world, it was in these smaller, seemingly frivolous situations where the Holy Spirit began to teach me the importance of trust and praying bold prayers. We had been traveling all night on a red-eye flight from Los Angeles to Houston, Texas. There were a number of elements that contributed to my bag getting lost that day, and among those were the fact that we had only just made our initial red-eye flight (with special thanks to LA traffic for delaying us and causing this predicament in the first place). We were working for a friend who was scheduled to speak at a corporate event in Houston the following morning and we had multiple boxes of his product with us to sell at the event, along with our own suitcases, all together totaling about 15 items of luggage. We arrived with less than 45 minutes until departure, and as you would expect there was pandemonium at the baggage check-in to ensure our entire fleet of luggage was secured on the flight in time. It was a miracle that the staff at LAX even checked our bags to begin with. In addition to this, we had to make a connection flight in Las Vegas, which meant that all of those bags had to be transferred onto our connecting flight. Upon arriving in Houston, dressed in my most comfortable tracksuit attire and looking a little worse for wear after having slept very little through the night on the two flights, we waited for our bags. I had this feeling in the pit of my stomach as I watched each and every bag and box slowly make their way out onto the conveyer belt. I just knew. My heart sank as the last bag tumbled out of the opening and the conveyer belt came to a stop.

I must stress the importance of this bag of mine. I was scheduled to be selling all of the products at a corporate event in just under a few hours, and within that bag was most of my makeup and business attire

RELEASING PROPHETIC SOLUTIONS

for the next few days. There was no way I could show up dressed as I was, and there was no time to go shopping to buy new clothes; we were driving straight from the airport to the event. To add to the problem, we were leaving this event at the end of the day and driving straight back to the airport to take our next flight for yet another corporate event scheduled in Florida the next day. I approached the lost bags counter and gave them the corresponding ticket for my suitcase and after about fifteen minutes of nail-biting suspense, they managed to track my luggage down and found it had been mistakenly kept in Las Vegas. The baggage handler was holding my luggage, and on speakerphone he read out the numbers on the tag, the exact corresponding numbers to the ticket that I had just handed over. I was then informed that they could not get the bag to me in Texas until two more days. By then, we would be in Arkansas and I would have to endure two full days of corporate events, dressed as I was, with no toiletries, no change of clothes, no makeup, no corporate wear, and no time to buy anything else. Both Nate and our two friends were sympathetic, but only my husband could read the extreme stress showing on my face. Our two friends were ready to move on, with tight schedules to meet weighing on their minds, and so they shrugged, "things will work out," and began walking toward the exit.

If you have ever lost a bag, you know the feeling. I felt defeated and frustrated at the prospect of the humiliation of selling products to high-profile business leaders basically dressed in the next best thing to pajamas. Right then I remembered a scripture my dad had often prayed whenever he had lost something—Mark 4:22. "*For there is nothing that is hidden that won't be disclosed, and there is no secret that won't be brought out into the light!*" I realize that scripture is speaking of spiritual matters, but I had seen my dad's words of faith cause it to manifest lost things in the natural as well. I felt the words of that scripture bubbling up within me. Suddenly, they burst out of me in a very loud outpouring of a heartfelt declaration, with tears streaming down my face in desperation. "Father God, Your Word says that if anything is hidden, You will bring it into the light. I know my bag is not lost, but it has been hidden from me, and I need it now. Father, I release Your angels to bring it to me in Jesus' name. Bag, you will return to me right now." It is amusing how we see things playing out in our own minds. As I was praying, I was hoping that somehow I would get a knock on our hotel room door in an hour or two, just in time for the event, but God's ways are so much better than ours.

Our two friends who were walking a few steps ahead of Nate and me turned and stared almost in disbelief when they heard me praying, with the look on their faces that read, "What on earth are you doing?" Not even a moment passed when all of a sudden, right in front of all of our eyes, the conveyer belt to the left of us that we happened to be walking past abruptly turned on and started to move, and right there at the mouth of where the bags emerge there appeared my bag. I didn't believe it was my bag at this point until it made its way right to where I was standing and the conveyer belt halted. I turned it over looking for my identifiable tag just to be sure and there it was. Our jaws dropped, and then loud laughter erupted from all four of us. I ran back to the lost bags counter and showed my suitcase to the lady who had just found it in Las Vegas, and she was just as shocked as all of us. "It's Jesus!" I shouted. "Jesus delivered my bag."

While it may seem insignificant or even petty that God would deliver a lost bag, it was important to me and it actually left me feeling overcome with His love for days to come. It was an act of love, the response of a loving Father who cares about the little details of my life, and He moved immediately in response to my impassioned decree. I didn't know it then, but the Holy Spirit was using moments like this one to train me in prophetic prayer in its simplest form. I cried out to my Father, I told Him my problem, and then I spoke the answer. I began to wonder, "God if You responded to something as little as my lost suitcase, how much more will You answer me when it involves the bigger things of life?" I began to see problems differently, both the smaller obstacles within my own life and then on a larger scale—the dilemmas of the world. I began to see them through the eyes of possibility when hand in hand with my Father.

I believe God's desire is to stir up your faith for the same thing, to pray bold prayers of prophetic declaration over the little and the big. To speak His answers into every circumstance that might look impossible, and to hear His heart for the earth and the problems it faces. For every problem, He has a solution—and it is found in His Son, Jesus. He is waiting on His sons and daughters, who have been given all of His authority, to partner with Him and release the answers of His heart to a broken world. If you will dare to pray the answers boldly, despite what it may appear to look like in the natural, He will respond, and when He does it will astound you.

UNVEILING GOD SOLUTIONS

In my earlier experiences of learning prophetic prayer, I discovered that they each involved something important that was lost, just like my lost suitcase. In this instance, the verse from Mark 4:22 came to my heart, and I want to highlight why. Let us take a moment to read that verse, along with the two verses that accompany it on either side. Mark 4:21-23 in the Passion Translation reads:

> *He also gave them this parable: "No one lights a lamp only to place it under a basket or under the bed. It is meant to be placed on a lampstand. For there is nothing that is hidden that won't be disclosed, and there is no secret that won't be brought out into the light! If you understand what I'm saying, you need to respond!"*

What was Jesus referring to when He mentioned hidden things? I believe that Proverbs 25:2 points us to the answer. It reads:

> *God conceals the revelation of his word in the hiding place of his glory. But the honor of kings is revealed by how they thoroughly search out the deeper meaning of all that God says.*

The Hebrew word for *word* mentioned here is *dabar* (Strong's, H1693). It can be translated to literally mean, "word, speech, utterance, or matter." So what are the hidden things Jesus was referring to and the revelation that God conceals? He conceals the answers for the earth within His Word. When we consider that Jesus is the Word made flesh (see John 1:14), we can know that the revelation for "matters and problems," along with the deeper insights of His kingdom, can be found within the hiding place of His glory—discovered through intimacy with Him. Jesus is the solution to every problem and matter. Who are the kings who thoroughly search out these deeper meanings? You and I are those kings (see Rev. 1:6). Jesus is the King of all kings; He is our Great Priest, and you have been established as a king under His rule and reign. For too long, many of God's sons and daughters have hidden their lamps and the answers of His heart and not released these solutions into the earth. It is His desire to restore that which has been lost, and He longs to do it through you and me. We are here to affect culture, not to be infected by it. A king or queen of the earth may live in their kingdom while reigning over it, but they live separate from it. You and I have been called to live in the same way, to live and reign over the earth, but to be separate to it. Why? The answers that you carry within you are vital to restoring heaven to earth and they cannot be infected by the mindsets of the earth. That is why God hides these answers, so that they can only be obtained in intimacy.

In relationship, the revelations and solutions you receive are then released into the earth through your utterance. Notice Jesus said in Mark 4:23, *"If you understand what I'm saying, you need to respond!"* Only those who dare to go beyond the normal status quo and enter into the secret place of His glory will be able to understand and hear the solutions of His heart and respond as such. What is the ultimate purpose of these solutions? To uncover those who have been lost and to bring them back into the arms of the Father. Every solution in the heart of God is designed with one purpose and outcome in mind—to unveil His glory and bring the lost home.

PROPHETIC SOLUTION KEY #1

Pray from victory.

Your prophetic prayers carry the authority of Jesus to usher in the answers of heaven ahead of time, just like the Roman officer. Have you been praying like the Roman officer? Or begging God to move? It's time to shift your perspective into the realm of extravagant and bold faith—to release the answers of heaven into the earth.

NOTES

1. Beni Johnson, *The Happy Intercessor* (Shippensburg, PA: Destiny Image Publishers, 2009), 39-40.

2. Dutch Sheets, *Authority in Prayer* (Bloomington, MN: Bethany House Publishers, 2006), 14.

CHAPTER TWO

THE WEAPON
IN YOUR HANDS

If you were to do a quick internet search to find the two most powerful words in the English language, you would be led to countless web pages, articles, videos, seminars, and inspirational quotes, many of which point almost unanimously to two particular words. Philosophers, psychologists, motivational speakers, university teachers, and doctors combined all say these two words have the power to alter the course and trajectory of your life, depending on how you use them. These two words are so powerful, in fact, that many motivational speakers have entire books, courses, and even seminars written on them. These two words are simply—*I am*. Do you recognize them? One of the names of God, the Great I AM. All of these worldly orators have a common quote that they use often:

> What you speak and believe after "I AM" will control
> your decisions and shape your life. —Source unknown

It is profound to me that even though they don't understand the true meaning of this Name, the world's greatest scholars recognize that the name of God is powerful. Their writings about these words, however, are not pointed toward God but self, and therein lies their problem. The world has become a self-made society, and even more so with the rise of social media where anyone can become a self-made superstar. The world's affection is founded upon the approval of man, and when your affection is turned toward their approval, you must live your life enslaved to fulfilling their desires. The world's wisdom says, "I am powerful in my own right. I am my own god." This is why it is common to see the brightest stars of this world fall into darkness as quickly as their names rose into lights. This trap is as old as satan himself, for when he was lucifer it is written about him in Isaiah 14:13-14:

> For you have said in your heart:
> "I will ascend into heaven,
> I will exalt my throne above the stars of God;
> I will also sit on the mount of the congregation on the far-thest sides of the north;
> I will ascend above the heights of the clouds,
> I will be like the Most High" (NKJV).

Lucifer desired to be *greater than* God, and we can see this desire at play in the world around us. The way of true wisdom, however, writes a different story for the lives of God's sons and daughters. You and I find our strength by being hidden in the Great I AM. The wisdom of God says, "I am powerful *in* the Great I AM." When our identity is firmly established inside of Him, we are able to effectively deploy His kingdom. How many times, however, do we flippantly use these words "I am" and place after them phrases like, "I am… only young," "I am…too old," "I am…not enough," "I am…not qualified," "I am…not equipped." This is a snare of the enemy to deconstruct who we really are in Christ. He knows that all authority has been placed into the hands of Jesus, who has then given this authority to you and me, and the only way he can gain any traction is by your agreement. If your words agree and align with his lies, you have essentially given the enemy a key to a padlock that holds you tightly in bondage to yourself. I know, because I lived in bondage to insecurity for the early years of my life. I remember my early years of childhood being happy and normal. I was outgoing, but also quiet and pensive. Only now do I look back and realize that even as a child, God had given me the gift of perception. I would feel atmospheres, whether heavy or light, and even as a little girl I remember feeling the pull of intercession for people. As such, I liked to observe, but that was very quickly perceived by people in a negative light, and I was often questioned: "Why are you so quiet?" "What's wrong with you?" "Cat got your tongue?" It is amazing how quickly a lie can take root, and before long one lie turns into another. If I look back at the timeline of my life, I can pinpoint that somewhere between the ages of eight and ten the lie that something was wrong with me had embedded itself deep into my heart. I began trying to seek the approval of people around me through performing. I enrolled in the school choir along with my friends, much to my reluctance. Even though I could hold a note, I wasn't gifted with song, and so I spent many miserable years in choir, all to gain the approval of my friends and the people around me.

Somewhere along the line I had believed the lie that I was not gifted enough, bold enough, or talented enough. Insecurity had wrapped itself around my heart like a rope suffocating every breath. It was many years later, when I walked through the valley of depression, where these lies began to surface. One at a time, the Holy Spirit unveiled His truth over each of them and uprooted them from my life. His wraparound presence became my breath, and I found life for the first time as I discovered who He is and found myself in Him. What has any of this got to do with prophetic prayer, you might ask? Knowing that your identity is not in the gift of prophetic prayer but in the One who gives this gift is equally if not more important than the gift itself. The enemy will look for any loophole he can get to unravel the power of prophecy and prayer, and one of the first places he will look is insecurity. When you surrender that weakness to God, however, He uses that very weakness and turns it into a weapon against the enemy.

DO NOT SAY "I AM ONLY..."

When I was around the age of 18, I was asked to do a personality test for a job application. You know the kind where you are required to honestly answer a hundred questions about yourself, and then at the end of the never-ending questionnaire you are finally given a detailed explanation of your personality. The results of this particular test left me wondering if someone had been sitting in my house and spying on me. How could this test tell me so much about myself? I felt a sense of pride as I read through the positive section, but as I got into the negative section my spirit quickly dropped like a big sack of flour onto the floor. Mess everywhere. As I read the lines, "intro-verted, stubborn, easily depressed, inclined to pessimism," it was as though they settled like a label over my mind and remained with me for many years to come. I began to identify with these apparent negatives, and while I would never say that being introverted is a negative, I began to disqualify myself from the very things God was calling me into based on the judgments of this one personality test. I had believed these lies so profoundly that when a prophetic man of God visited our church and prophesied over me in my early twenties, I don't even remember the prophecy. If it wasn't for my then-fiancé, Nate, who just so happened to be standing next to me as it played out, I would to this day have no idea what was said.

I was standing up near the sound desk of our church, and as any pastor's kid can probably recall, my family and I were always first to the church and last to leave. This particular day we had a visiting speaker from America, one whom I had grown up admiring and lis-tening to. In the early afternoon hours before anyone else arrived, I had gone to church with my dad so that he could welcome our visitor, but my real reason was so I could meet with Nate and chat before the service. As Nate and I were sitting at the back of the auditorium, my dad had just welcomed the visiting minister, Dr. Jerry Savelle, and together they were walking past us toward the green room. As they walked by Nate and me, Dr. Jerry said a quick hello and continued on his way, but then he stopped, turned around, and walked back to me. I say this, recounting the words from my now-husband, because while I can remember this aspect of it, I still cannot remember his exact words. Jerry looked at me sternly in the eyes and said, "God has anointed you as a prophet to the nations. You will carry His voice to the ends of the earth." Apparently, I looked at him flabbergasted, and with cheeks blushing I blurted out, "You can't possibly mean me?" To which he responded, "God has spoken it." And off he went.

I wanted to ask you today—how many times have you questioned the call of God upon your life? Have you, like me, convinced yourself otherwise? Have you told yourself that your personality doesn't allow for it? Have you told yourself that you've been through too much, you've done too much wrong, or that you aren't qualified? I want to repeat the same words of God in the Garden of Eden, when He was speaking to Adam and Even immediately after the fall: *"Who told you that you were naked? Have you eaten from the tree that I commanded you not to eat from?"* (Gen. 3:11 NIV). I believe the Spirit of God is this day asking you the same question: "Who told you that you were not enough? Have you been eating from the tree of lies?" When God called the prophet Jeremiah, He spoke a magnificent declaration over his life, which you are likely familiar with. In Jeremiah 1:4-5, He says, *"The word of the Lord came to me, saying: 'Before I formed you in the womb I knew you, and before you were born I set you apart and appointed you as a prophet to the nations'"* (BSB).

This same declaration is true for you today. God, the maker of the heavens and the earth, formed you in the womb; He knew you before the foundations of the earth. He specifically chose you for this day and this age and He has called you forth, set you apart, and appointed you to prophesy His will over the nations. In the New Testament, we are *all* called to prophesy (see Acts 2:17), not just those who operate in the office of a prophet. We are *all* called to speak His heart over the nations, but too many of us question this calling. We question if we are enough. We compare ourselves one to another rather than hiding inside the security of who He is. I want to show you that you are not alone. Jeremiah also felt the insecurity arise; he replied to the Lord after this beautiful declaration and said, *"'Ah, Lord God,' I said, 'I surely do not know how to speak, for I am only a child!'"* (Jer. 1:6 BSB). Did you catch those words in there? *I am only a child.* This is a centuries-old insecurity. It didn't start with you, but it ends with Jesus. Listen to the Lord's reply to Jeremiah and, consequently, to you also:

> *But the Lord told me: "Do not say,*
> *'I am only a child.'*
> *For to everyone I send you,*
> *you must go, and all that I command you,*
> *you must speak.*
> *Do not be afraid of them,*
> *for I am with you to deliver you,"*
> *declares the Lord*
> (Jeremiah 1:7-8 BSB).

Did you notice there that God first confronted the lie—"do not say I am only a child"—and then secured the calling of Jeremiah with Himself by saying, "for I AM with you to deliver you." He called Jeremiah to prophesy and speak, not based on Jeremiah's merits but His. Likewise, you have been called and appointed to release the prophetic solutions of His heart into the earth, not based on your merits but on His. I believe the Father is saying to you today, beloved son or daughter, "Do not say, 'I am only...' for I have called you. I have set you apart this day, in this terrain, to be My mouthpiece of glory. Do not be afraid of them, for I AM with you and I will deliver you." The next verses of Jeremiah 1 are amazing; it is where Jeremiah's mouth is anointed to prophesy. First, the lies must be removed, then the truth is revealed. It is upon His authority that we move and speak into the nations, and when our identity is in Him, He anoints our words and fulfills His mandate upon the earth.

> *Then the Lord reached out His hand, touched my mouth, and said to me:*
> *"Behold, I have put My words into your mouth.*
> *See, I have appointed you today*
> *over nations and kingdoms*
> *to uproot and tear down,*
> *to destroy and overthrow,*
> *to build and plant"*
> (Jeremiah 1:9-10 BSB).

My friends, it does not matter to Him how many times you have failed or what kind of personality you have. This is not the end of your story; this is a new chapter written by His hands, with His anointing dripping upon every page of your life. All that is required of you is simple surrender into what He has spoken over you. There is no need to question how, for it is on the authority of His Word that all of His works are finished and completed. God is rewriting your story, but your story is not just about you; He will rewrite your story to rewrite others. I have watched in my own life how God has taken the very insecurities and weaknesses that I thought would ruin me, and He has filled me with Himself and turned the very things the enemy once used to his advantage and caused them to become weapons of mass destruction against satan. When I said, "How could I ever be a mouthpiece for God when I am terrified of speaking in front of others?" I have watched how God has invaded that weakness and filled it with His courage. I have watched how this little introvert who was terrified of public speaking now loves to speak because every time I get up it is in complete dependency upon Him, and He has never left me alone. He has always met me when I stepped out and it has been His power that has surged through me and strengthened me in my weakness. God is not defined by my weakness and He is certainly not defined by yours. For when the Great I AM fills you, you will release who He is into every sphere of influence around you, just as Second Corinthians 12:9-11 describes;

> *But he answered me, "My grace is always more than enough for you, and my power finds its full expression through your weakness." So I will celebrate my weaknesses, for when I'm weak I sense more deeply the mighty power of Christ living in me. So I'm not defeated by my weakness, but delighted! For when I feel my weakness and endure mistreatment— when I'm surrounded with troubles on every side and face persecution because of my love for Christ—I am made yet stronger. For my weakness becomes a portal to God's power.*

PROPHECY IS A WEAPON

I often see many Christians running from place to place in search of their next prophetic word. In fact, it is the question I am asked more often than any other: "Do you have a prophetic word for me?" While there is absolutely nothing wrong with searching for the prophetic word of the Lord for our lives—in fact, I strongly encourage it—oftentimes what we tend to forget is we already have been given a prophetic word that we have done nothing with. On the flip side of that, you will usually find that the prophetic word of God is so big that we don't know where to start so we "shelve it" until we can figure out what to do with it. In the meantime, we search for something else. Unless the Lord highlights a specific word to me for others, I will usually ask people, "What was the last prophetic word you received?" More often than not, they received a word last week, last month, or last year that they have done nothing with. Sometimes it is because of the insecurities I mentioned above, and other times it is out of disappointment of not yet seeing that word fulfilled that we shelve it. Or, on the other hand, it is not knowing how to use the prophecies as weapons in our lives. Again, this is something I have learned through trial and error. I consider myself to be in an ongoing, continual training in this particular area. It is important that we know how to wage war with the prophecies for our own lives, based on the merit of who He is in us and through us; otherwise, we won't know how to wage war with the prophecies He gives us over nations.

In August of 2011, I had picked up a book from our local Christian bookstore that I had no idea would change the course of my life. I had a two-month-old newborn at home and was simply looking for something to read in the night hours when Charlotte would wake for her almost hourly feeds or diaper changes. (Both of my girls were born as movers and shakers right from the time they were in the womb, and it was evident as newborns they were not prepared to sleep through the night, much to my delight.) I needed something to keep me awake and I came across a newly released book called *Unplanned* by Abby Johnson. You may be familiar with its movie counterpart released the same year at the time of this writing. When the book was released, however, there was very little talk in that day about the book's main focal point—abortion. A recent experience where my own niece was almost aborted, however, had led me to buy this book out of interest and read it.

In the early morning hours of that month, I began reading the first chapters. I remember being so overcome with emotion that each time I read it, I would put my sleeping newborn back into her cot and I couldn't go back to sleep. I would go into a separate room so as not to wake my husband and cry out in grief to God. It was particularly emotional for me as I had just birthed this beautiful little baby who lay asleep in my arms. It was during this time that the Holy Spirit also began to wake me in the night (I didn't get much sleep in that season of my life) with an intense groaning. I'll never forget the first time it happened. I was in a deep sleep and suddenly woke up with the overpowering presence of His Spirit upon me. It was so overwhelming, in a good way, all I could do was groan. The only thing I can liken it to is the groans of childbirth—without the physical pain. Whenever this would happen, I could hear the Spirit of God whispering to my heart, "I am calling you to intercede over abortion. I am calling you to prophesy the end of this evil." The Bible calls this kind of intercession *travailing prayer*. I had no idea about travailing, and I had little understanding of prophecy or intercession at this point in my life, but I knew God was calling me to pray.

I also had no knowledge of "waging war with prophecy" as Paul instructs Timothy in First Timothy 1:19: *"With this encouragement use your prophecies as weapons as you wage spiritual warfare by faith and with a clean conscience. For there are many who reject these virtues and are now destitute of the true faith."* All I knew to do was to write down the words the Holy Spirit had spoken to me in those early hours and search in my Bible for a promise that confirmed it. I immediately found a scripture that I knew was a prophetic weapon for me regarding this issue, and any time that the matter arose in my heart I declared the answer. I decreed the Name of Jesus over abortion and spoke the scripture. I didn't know it then, but I was waging war with the prophecy He had given me.

Later, that prophecy would require further action from me, but for now this was moving more in the supernatural than I could possibly comprehend. Only recently, I found a timeline that was published by a leading abortion provider in America depicting the dates when opposition to their right to kill unborn babies had amplified. I was astounded when I saw one of the first dates—it was the very month that the Holy Spirit spoke to me. I'm not suggesting I was alone in those prayers. I know it was the culmination of many prayers from many people all over the world (and I know it will require the culmination of ongoing prayer to completely defeat), but I knew God allowed me to see the date to show me just how effective my obedience to prophetic prayer is.

God will always call you to something that is much bigger than you. That is exactly what He did in those early morning hours in 2011. He marked my life for something much greater than me, something that I would have to learn how to lean into Him for, learn how to hide myself in His presence with, something that would require my identity to be completely secure in Him and who He says He is. If you are reading this, then, there is no doubt in my mind that He has marked your life for something bigger than you as well. It just may be that He has called you to pray to see the end of abortion as well, or it could be something entirely different. Whatever it is, you can be certain that God has called you when you look at the size of the problem and the size of yourself and realize, "There is no way I can do this on my own." That is when you know it is Him. The question is, what do you do with the calling once it is given to you? I want to continue to show you how to wage war with the prophecies and callings God has given you.

WHAT IS IN YOUR HANDS?

When God called and appointed Moses to deliver the entire nation of Israel from the hands of a tyrant ruler in Egypt, Moses must have been taken aback. We all know the story, but I want you to consider the connotations of the position Moses was in when God called forth his destiny. He had killed a man and was likely living with the guilt of that murder as we find Moses had been in hiding out in the desert. For nearly forty years, he was living in a place called Midian, which can be translated to mean "strife" (Strong's, H4092). Regardless of the place of weakness he was in, God called him.

In Exodus 3, we read about the encounter Moses has with God in the midst of the burning bush, and God says to him in verse 10, *"Come now therefore, and I will send you to Pharaoh, that you may bring forth My people, the Israelites, out of Egypt"* (AMPC). Picture yourself as Moses for a moment. Would you have jumped up and said, "Yes, I'll do it. I've been hiding because I killed a man, and even though I've been living in the land of strife, yes, I am certainly qualified to deliver millions of people out of the hands of the tyranny of Egypt." I know that if that was me, I would have likely crumpled under the weight of the calling, as Moses did at first. For he replied in verse 11, *"Who am I, that I should go to Pharaoh and bring the Israelites out of Egypt?"* (AMPC). I love the sweet words of reassurance and the conversation that ensues between God and Moses in the following verses.

> *God said, I will surely be with you; and this shall be the sign to you that I have sent you: when you have brought the people out of Egypt, you shall serve God on this mountain [Horeb, or Sinai]* (Exodus 3:12 AMPC).

As you will discover in chapters to come, we are called to ascend mountains. Isn't it amazing that the sign that He was with Moses is Moses would serve Him on the mountain? Horeb or Sinai can mean "to lay waste" (Strong's, H2722). Lay waste to what? Lay waste to the slavery of the Israelites. In other words, you and I are called to conquer mountains by laying waste to the enemy's plans and then worship the Lord from the victory. Moses, who was still not entirely convinced in this conversation, asks the Lord:

> *Behold, when I come to the Israelites and say to them, The God of your fathers has sent me to you, and they say to me, What is His name? What shall I say to them?* (Exodus 3:13 AMPC)

God's answer to him is profound. He says:

> *I AM WHO I AM and WHAT I AM, and I WILL BE*
> *WHAT I WILL BE; and He said, You shall say this to the*
> *Israelites: I AM has sent me to you! God said also to Moses,*
> *This shall you say to the Israelites: The Lord, the God of*
> *your fathers, of Abraham, of Isaac, and of Jacob, has sent*
> *me to you! This is My name forever, and by this name I*
> *am to be remembered to all generations* (Genesis 3:14-15
> AMPC).

It is the first mention where God calls Himself "I AM." Personally perplexed by what "I AM" means, I began to do an extensive study on its Hebrew origins and what it means. I looked up all the mentions of "I AM" throughout the Bible. In every single instance where "I AM" is mentioned, it is always in reference to His great authority, magnificence, and power. Jesus fulfilled these words and spoke them numerous times throughout the Gospels, and in John 14:6 He reassured His disciples before going to the cross by saying, *"I am the way, the truth, and the life. No one comes to the Father except through me"* (NIV). His name, I AM, speaks of His fullness and the entirety of His person.

When I looked up the Hebrew meaning of this name, I discovered that it means (drumroll please) I AM. I was kind of hoping for some elaborate explanation, but then the revelation came to me. This name encompasses *all* that He is and *all* that He has. When God calls you, He has the reputation of calling you to do great and mighty works, not because of what you can do but because of what He can do. He doesn't do things in halves, and nor does He do anything with small-minded and limited thinking. You are reading these pages not by coincidence or accident; it is because He has called you and equipped you based on the fullness and the entirety of who He is. If God called you to do something little, it would insult the greatness of His name. He has called you based on the merits of I AM. Which means that you can be confident in this, that He who has started a good work in you is faithful to finish it (see Phil. 1:6 NIV). He has appointed you, like Moses, to release the prophetic solutions of His heart into the nations for His purposes, to emancipate the lost and deliver them into His kingdom. It all starts with a spoken word of God, and from that word His will is ushered into the earth. Pay attention to the words that come from your mouth. Are you still saying things like, "I am...not enough, not equipped, not gifted"? It is time to change those words based on the merit of who He is and start saying, "I am called, anointed, appointed, set apart, and chosen, and I am well able, because He who has called me is the Great I AM, and He is faithful to complete what He began in me."

You may still be asking God, like Moses did, "But how Lord? Where do I begin?" Moses' internal struggle to believe that God had called him to such a mighty display of God's power was still apparent in Exodus 4 where he says to God that he doubts the Israelites will even believe him. Maybe you still doubt how it could be possible that God will work through you. God didn't acknowledge Moses' insecurity; instead, He revealed to Moses a weapon that was already in his hands. God said to him in Exodus 4:2, "What is that in your hand, Moses?" And he said, "A rod." I believe God, who is the same yesterday, today, and forever, is speaking the same thing to you today, friend. He is not moved by your insecurity or your apparent lack of qualifications, but He is asking you, "What is in your hand?" The weapon of His Word is already in your hand. The question is, will you use it? Will you use it to strike down the enemy's plans over your life? Will you use it to overturn satan's grasp over regions and nations? Will you use the authority that has been paid with precious Blood for you to wield?

Far too many of God's sons and daughters are walking around with this rod of authority in their hands, the power of the Great I AM, and instead of using it they are talking themselves out of the very destiny God has assigned to them. They are telling themselves based on the premise of their insecurities and qualifications that they do not have what it takes. I am here to remind you, today, what is already in your hands is more powerful than you realize. Many people see Moses' rod as a simple walking aid, a staff to walk with, but the word for *rod* in Hebrew, *matteh* (Strong's, H4294), can be translated to mean a scepter of authority. Though it may have looked like a simple walking staff, it was actually a symbol of God's anointing upon Moses to walk in the destiny he was called to. In ancient Hebrew times, a *matteh*, or a rod, was metaphorically the image of abundant supply, strength, and authority. Revelation 19:15-16 says, *"A sharp sword came from his mouth with which to conquer the nations, and he will shepherd them with an iron scepter. He will trample out the wine in the winepress of the wrath of God. On his robe and on his thigh he had inscribed a name: King of kings and Lord of lords."*

Jesus is the rod of your authority. He is the scepter you have the privilege to wield. You and I have been given the task to shepherd the nations, to deploy our words with prophetic utterances that will release His kingdom into the earth. Upon the authority of the Great I AM, you have been deployed into the earth for such a time as this.

PROPHETIC SOLUTIONS KEY #2

Pray with the rod of your authority.

Your strongest weapon against the enemy is the Great I AM. Have you been discrediting His ability to work in you and through you? Ask the Holy Spirit to reveal to you how He sees you and proclaim this over yourself, "It is not by might, nor by power, but by His Spirit" (see Zech. 4:6 NIV).

CHAPTER THREE

THE WATCHMAN
AND THE
GATEKEEPERS

In the year of 2017, I began to see the word *gatekeeper* everywhere. It started when Nate, our two girls, and I were visiting the rustic town of Hobart in Tasmania, Australia for a ministry trip. We were having a family day off from ministry together to explore the historical city, and we accidently stumbled upon an old "Gatekeepers Cottage" in Hobart's idyllic Botanical Gardens. Built in 1845, the small cottage had become a little museum of sorts and I knew something about it was significant, so I went inside to explore. The strange thing was, as soon as I stepped in through the front door, I felt a physical chill go through my spine. Our girls must have felt the same unsettled eeriness as they both quickly ran straight back out the front door. I immediately began to pray; I knew my authority and so I was still determined to see what was on the inside that I felt the Holy Spirit wanted to show me. As I prayed and walked through, I read the historical stories displayed on the wall and it became quickly evident what I was meant to see. There were recorded facts of "ghosts" (we know them to be demons) that had appeared to the gatekeepers who lived in this little cottage. These ghost-demons had haunted the inhabitants of the cottage and eventually took possession of it by driving them out and making it unlivable. As soon as I read that, the Holy Spirit spoke to my heart, "When a Gatekeeper does not take up the authority of his or her post, a violation occurs where the enemy sees a vacant position, invades that position, and takes over."

When I received this insight from the Holy Spirit, I didn't have much knowledge then about the spiritual significance of gatekeepers, so I began researching and studying their meaning. I was amazed to find that there is a wealth of information in scripture about gatekeepers and I want to share some of my findings with you. You may be wondering what on earth a gatekeeper is. A gatekeeper is exactly as it sounds—one who protects a territory by standing guard at its gate or entrance. We know Jesus to be the Gate, so evidently it is His kingdom we are guarding on the earth. When you pray prophetic prayers, you are like a guard standing ground over the regions of the earth and ensuring that no enemy can invade the borders of your assigned region. I honestly believe that the reason the world is in the fragile state that it is in at the time of writing this book is because far too many of God's sons and daughters have not occupied their gates. I have had many a conversation with brothers and sisters in Christ who have told me, "Well, Isaiah 60:2 says that darkness shall cover the earth, so what is the point of praying?" I like to remind them that they have forgotten the entirety of those verses, which say:

Rise up in splendor and be radiant, for your light has dawned,

and Yahweh's glory now streams from you!

Look carefully! Darkness blankets the earth,

and thick gloom covers the nations,

but Yahweh arises upon you

and the brightness of his glory appears over you!

Nations will be attracted to your radiant light

and kings to the sunrise-glory of your new day.

Lift up your eyes higher! Look all around you and believe,

for your sons are returning from far away

and your daughters are being tenderly carried home.

Watch as they all gather together, eager to come back to you!

(Isaiah 60:1-4)

When we take up our rightful positions of authority upon the earth, we will see the fulfillment of this promise. In many ways we are seeing the fulfillment of only one portion of this verse, *"darkness blankets the earth, and thick gloom covers the nations,"* and I believe it is time to see the fulfillment of the entirety of it. Darkness cannot outshine light, and the presence of darkness only means you have the opportunity to shine brighter. So, let's get to shining. Let's take up our positions as gatekeepers upon the earth and drive out the darkness by shining His light and standing guard over what God is doing. As you decree, light comes forth through your spoken words. As you pray, God responds. I want to continue to show you the amazing role of the gatekeeper in scripture.

THE DUTIES OF A GATEKEEPER

In the Old Testament, the role of the gatekeeper fell to the tribe of Levites. They were assigned the roles of both priests and guards/gatekeepers for the temple. In First Chronicles 26 it details the duties of the gatekeepers. In verses 13-16, we are given an account of the names of families who were assigned to each gate guarding the temple.

> *They were assigned by families for guard duty at the various gates, without regard to age or training, for it was all decided by means of sacred lots.*
> *The responsibility for the east gate went to Meshelemiah and his group. The north gate was assigned to his son Zechariah, a man of unusual wisdom. The south gate went to Obed-edom, and his sons were put in charge of the storehouse. Shuppim and Hosah were assigned the west gate and the gateway leading up to the Temple* (1 Chronicles 26:13-16 NLT).

While that may seem like a group of difficult-to-pronounce names, there is a hidden message in their meanings. I'll break it down for you:

- To the North gate was assigned *Zechariah*. His name means "Yahweh Remembers" (Strong's, H2142, 3050).

- To the South gate was assigned *Obed-edom*. His name means "servant of the red one." The "red one" is prophetic symbolism pointing to Jesus (Strong's, H5654).

- To the East Gate was assigned *Meshelemiah*. His name means "the Lord repays" (Strong's, H4920).

- To the West Gate was assigned *Shuppim* and *Hosah*. Their names mean "to mark a border" or "door keeper" and "to seek refuge" (Strong's, H8206, 2621).

When we put those name meanings together, it reads, *"Yahweh remembers the servant of the red one (Jesus.) The Lord repays those who mark their border and seek refuge in Him."*

God is saying to you and me—who are called to guard the lives of our families, cities, and nations through prophetic prayer, which, I believe, is the assignment of every child of God—that He remembers your sacrifice and service to Jesus. He repays you for your work of guarding your territory and seeking refuge in Him. It's also a beautiful picture of marking your territory with the Blood of the Lamb. While an animal marks its territory with urine, we mark our borders spiritually on the earth with the Blood of Jesus, the red one. When God charged the Israelites to mark their doors with the blood of a sacrificed lamb in order that the spirit of death would pass over their homes, it was a prophetic picture of the coming Passover Lamb and what would then be available to those of us under the New Covenant. Through the New Covenant, we have been given the authority of the Lamb of God to mark the borders of His kingdom by His Blood.

How do we stand as gatekeepers in this modern day and age? By marking the borders of our assigned territory with His Blood through our decrees. I do this often when I am driving around. I decree over my neighborhoods that they are covered by the Blood of Jesus. When I am driving past schools in my area, I decree the protecting Blood of the Lamb over those schools. I command angels to stand guard over the schools and that no terror or harm will come to the children or their teachers there. I pray over shopping centers and decree that my city is a city covered in the Blood of Jesus and flooded with the presence of God. I prophesy regularly over my nation that mine is a nation that protects the sanctity of life. Just as the Israelites painted their doorways, I paint the doorways of my neighborhoods and everywhere I go with the powerful, atoning, protecting, and transforming Blood of Jesus. Whenever I do that, the enemy sees it, and he has no choice but to pass over a territory that is out of his jurisdiction. I refuse to allow my domain to become like that little cottage that was violated and overrun by an unlawful enemy.

GATEWAYS OF GLORY

I want to share with you a vision I had a year ago over the United States of America. Regardless of what country you are from, I believe this vision is significant for each of us to recognize the importance of standing guard over our family, over culture, over regions and nations. Whether you read this book when it is released or a hundred years from now, the prophetic decree remains true, so I encourage you to receive it over yourself and take up arms as a gatekeeper of God's kingdom.

In October of 2018, I wrote:

> There is a war on the gates of America right now, and that war is manifesting in the natural because of what

is happening in the supernatural. I believe the current political war that we are seeing play out is a mirror of this underlying spiritual war. I have been sensing a strong and undeniable urgency in recent days, like an ongoing alarm from the Spirit of God that the Gatekeepers must awaken. The prophetic intercessors must arise and take their place in this hour. I keep hearing the Holy Spirit's urgent impression to my heart, "There is a fierce battle waging at the gates of America, and the United States is in urgent need of *increased* and *intentional* intercession right now."

I believe the enemy's war on the gates of America is to gain unrestricted access to influence the world. I saw a vision of a monumental war at the spiritual gateway of America and it looked like the Golden Gate Bridge. Standing on one side of the bridge was an assault of demonic principalities, screaming and beating their chests in an attempt to scare their way into unrestricted access across the gate's barricades. On the other side of the bridge was an army of angels, assigned by heaven to stand guard and prevent this assault from crossing.

The angels were standing alongside gatekeepers (intercessors, prayer warriors) and were awaiting their commands and instruction. However, while there were many of these gatekeepers who were awake, many were also asleep. As the vision progressed, the assault on the other side of the bridge became more violent and agitated, and while the armed guard of angels were able to keep them at bay, I noticed they were not as effective as warring them off as they could have been had their sleeping gatekeepers been on guard and awake. It was as though they were helpless to be completely effective until every gatekeeper was awake. I believe the Lord showed me that vision to issue an urgent call to the church, and specifically to the gatekeepers and those called to intercede for America, that it is time to *awaken* from slumber and *move* in the authority given to you against this demonic onslaught.

Lifting the Fatigue

Last month I was asking the Lord to reveal the source of a myriad of witchcraft attacks that we had been enduring all year. I was tired and worn out after constantly finding our daily lives interrupted with swirling confusion, frustration, and odd circumstances. The Holy Spirit then led me to this scripture:

For he has strengthened the authority of your gates. He even blesses you with more children. He's the one who brings peace to your borders, feeding you the most excellent of fare (Psalm 147:13-14).

Within a matter of days, the enemy's sly and crafty plans behind all of the attacks were revealed and we were able to see a swift end to this relentless warfare. As the dust settled, I was able to clearly see that the confusion that had been surrounding us had caused me to "sleep" in many ways through warfare. It was a demonic strategy to exhaust me into a deep slumber. In fact, even my physical sleep had been affected. I was unable to sleep properly at night, and therefore I was physically tired and worn out during the day. I believe that many of those who are called to the front lines of intercession, those who have been given the keys of a nation as a gatekeeper, have been enduring this same onslaught of warfare—surrounded by a myriad of confusion, you have found yourself tired, exhausted, and asleep on the battlefield. I prophesy an end to these attacks in the name of Jesus. I decree that every sly and crafty assignment that has been sent your way to lull you into a slumber will be swiftly brought to an end. Where God promised me, He is promising you that He is strengthening the authority of your gates, and out of this onslaught of battles that you have been enduring you will see an increase in multiplication and fruition in your life. Not only will your life prosper, but He will also cause your intercession to prosper.

I believe I also need to prophesy this scripture over you, and I feel you need to also *shout* it out loud over yourself, like a clarion awakening call.

For the light makes everything visible. This is why it is said, "Awake, O sleeper, rise up from the dead, and Christ will give you light" (Ephesians 5:14 NLT).

I decree that the shining light of the Son will shine upon you and every darkness that has tried to surround you will dissipate in His brightness. Even as you read this, I believe you will feel a supernatural strengthening to awaken you and cause you to stand once again with renewed strength and *clarity*. It is time to take up your shield again, and I command an end to the onslaughts you have endured in Jesus' name. The enemy is powerless to withstand you, for you are needed on the front lines.

Taking Back the Enemy Lines

I kept hearing this phrase *lines of contention*. Intrigued by that statement, I did a search online trying to see if there was any biblical connection to this phrase. Instead, I found a prophetic language for what is happening. The first thing that comes up is in respect to broadband contention ratios. Basically speaking, a contention ratio is in reference to how many users are sharing the same broadband capacity on a line. To explain it even more simply, it is the count of how many households are using the same main broadband line. If a line of contention ratio is 20:1, it means twenty households are using the same broadband line.

Immediately I knew what the Holy Spirit was speaking through this. Currently, there is a contention in the spirit for the contention lines. The enemy is attempting to advance in ratio and outweigh what God is doing in America and the nations; however, God is calling the gatekeepers to be the higher ratio. I believe at this very moment in time, however, there is an imbalance. With many gatekeepers who have been asleep, the enemy's ratios are threatening to outweigh our own. Yet, as the gatekeepers respond to the clarion call, awakening and arising together using the same "lines" of authority, they will together advance and take back the enemy lines in a swift show of God's authority and power. It is *imperative* that the gatekeepers *arise*.

Make no mistake, the current spiritual war on the gates of America is because the enemy is in a frenzy to take back lost ground. He is losing his footing. The gatekeepers must maintain their authority on the frontlines, and as they do we will see these strongholds of giants fall, and *swiftly*.

You Hold the Keys

Take up your position, for God is strengthening the authority of your gates. He is strengthening the gates of America (and your nation) through you. The gates of hell shall not prevail against the armies of the Lord, and together we decree and declare that satan shall not possess your gates, your family's gates, your city's gates, the gates of America and your own nation, nor shall he possess the land.

I am here to call you back to the front lines, warrior friends. The enemy fears what you carry, he fears the authority you walk in, but the Lord's promise to you today as you step back up on the wall as a watchman is to bring peace to your borders, feeding you the most excellent of His fare. Let's together see this battle won for the glory of God.

Blessed is the man who listens to me, watching daily at my gates, waiting at the posts of my doors. For whoever finds me finds life, and obtains favor from the Lord (Proverbs 8:34-35 NKJV).[1]

THE WATCHMAN

You have likely heard the name *watchman* a lot as well. In biblical times, the watchman was a prophet and they were stationed in a watchtower, positioned up high so that they could see an incoming threat before anyone else. Likewise, in modern times God's prophets and His prophetic anointing work in the same way. He often reveals dreams, visions, or impressions to convey either a warning of the enemy's plans or His good intentions for the earth. It's easy to determine what His intentions are for the earth by simply asking yourself this question: "Is it good? Then it is His heart. Is it bad? Then it's a plan of the enemy God has revealed to me to overthrow." As it says in Acts 2:17, *"This is what I will do in the last days—I will pour out my Spirit on everybody and cause your sons and daughters to prophesy, and your young men will see visions, and your old men will experience dreams from God."* God uses the language of prophecy, visions, and dreams to pour out His Spirit. Which is why prophetic prayer is such a powerful weapon in this day and age. It is the merging of the watchman (prophecy) with the gatekeeper (prayer). When these two mantles rest upon the sons and daughters, it not only evicts the enemy from a region but unlocks the gates for God's Spirit to flow through.

In Isaiah 21:8 it says, *"And [the watchman] cried like a lion, O Lord, I stand continually on the watchtower in the daytime, and I am set in my station every night"* (AMPC). This assignment of prophetic prayer is a stationing, a positioning, a calling from God to occupy a territory and establish His kingdom there. I firmly believe that as the mantle of the watchman and the gatekeepers come together in prophetic prayer, releasing the intention of the Lord into the nations, we will see the fulfillment of Isaiah 60. As watchmen and gatekeepers, we hold the keys to keep the doors shut to the enemy, and also the keys to open wide the gates of the kingdom of heaven into the earth.

> *I will place on his shoulder the key to the house of David; what he opens no one can shut, and what he shuts no one can open* (Isaiah 22:22 NIV).

GATEWAYS OF PRAYER

Psalm 24:9 is such a powerful verse that speaks of both instruction for receiving and releasing the prophetic solutions of His kingdom into the earth. It says, *"So wake up, you living gateways, and rejoice! Fling wide, you ageless doors of destiny! Here he comes; the King of Glory is ready to come in."* The Hebrew text for this verse literally says, "lift up your heads, O gates." The Hebrew word for *head* is *rasekem* (Strong's, H7218), and it is defined as summit, head, or mountaintop. The Hebrew word for *gates* is *shar* (Strong's, H8179), and it means gate, entrance, meeting place, court of tabernacle, and heaven. Your head—your mind—is designed to be both the meeting place of His glory and the gateway for His kingdom. In the New Covenant, you are the living tabernacle, and God desires to deliver the answers and solutions that the earth is in need of through you. When your mind is set apart as a place of worship, it becomes a weapon and a gateway for the King of Glory to come through you into the earth. His solutions are released through the mountaintop and you are given the key to conquer mountains.

PROPHETIC SOLUTION KEY #3

Pray in the secret place.

As you enter into the secret place with Jesus, He transforms you into a living gateway, a gatekeeper and watchman over your family, your city, and your nation. The solutions of God come through you.

NOTE

1. Prophetic word taken from nateandchristy.co.

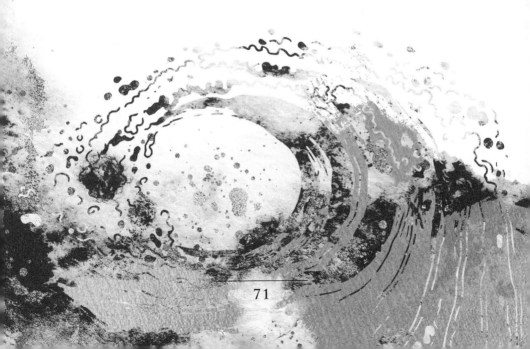

PART TWO

STRATEGIZING WITH GOD

CHAPTER FOUR

GOD SOLUTIONS

Call to me and I will answer you and tell you great and
unsearchable things you do not know (Jeremiah 33:3 NIV).

We were standing on the edge of a lookout overlooking
the bay area of San Francisco and the Golden Gate
Bridge in California. It is a beautiful sight to behold
where you can see the endless trail of cars streaming across the
majestic bridge, the rushing rivers of current within the ocean bay
below, the mound of Alcatraz Island in the middle of the bay, and
the far-stretching hills of San Francisco in the distance. Nate and
I had been traveling up California from Los Angeles, partly on a
mission of prayer from God and partly on a family holiday (although
I'm not entirely sure it could be called a holiday when you have a
very determined two-year-old and a limit-testing five-year-old in
tow). As I surveyed the beauty of San Francisco before me, my heart
grew suddenly sad. I began to feel the weight of the Father's longing
for this state and this city.

I want to stop here for a moment, because this is where many people get stuck. They feel the pain of the Father's heart over a person,

city, or region and pray from that place of pain; or rather, they pray what they see with their natural eyes. What do I mean by that? It is good to feel the pain of the Father's heart over a situation—that is the mark of intimacy and even intercession—but here is where we get to lean into Him further and ask Him what His intentions are. I like to ask Him, "What do You see beyond this current pain I see, Father? What is Your heart intention for this person or place that You love? What was the picture You had in mind when you created them?" We must learn to pray into the answers He sees. When Jesus was prophesying about His betrayer at the last supper, it says:

> Then Jesus was moved deeply in his spirit. Looking at his disciples, he announced, "I tell you the truth—one of you is about to betray me." Eyeing each other, his disciples puzzled over which one of them could do such a thing. The disciple that Jesus dearly loved was at the right of him at the table and was leaning his head on Jesus. Peter gestured to this disciple to ask Jesus who it was he was referring to. Then the dearly loved disciple leaned into Jesus' chest and whispered, "Master, who is it?" "The one I give this piece of bread to after I've dipped it in the bowl," Jesus replied (John 13:21-26).

It is the lovers of God, those who lean in close to Him, who are the ones entrusted to ask the questions and are given the secrets of His heart. John could have made an assumption and pointed the finger at any number of the disciples, but instead he asked. John was one of the three who was taken up to the mountain where Jesus was transfigured before their eyes. Even though Peter was with him,

Peter evidently still had issues when it came to trust. If he hadn't, he likely would not have ended up in the situation where he betrayed Jesus with his words just hours later. John was the one disciple who endured the horrors of the cross, remaining at the side of Jesus to the end. Why? He had become accustomed to abiding in His presence, and in doing so he had grown confident in his identity as a son of God. As a result, he was comfortable to lean on Jesus and confidently ask Him difficult questions. This kind of boldness is necessary if we are to effectively walk in prophetic prayer and release His solutions in the earth. *"So now we come freely and boldly to where love is enthroned, to receive mercy's kiss and discover the grace we urgently need to strengthen us in our time of weakness"* (Heb. 4:16).

Abiding in His presence gives us bold courage to come before Him, not in timidity. I used to do this—I would come before Him timidly and beg Him to help me. "Oh, please help me. Please help this situation I am in. Please do something." While there is nothing wrong with asking for His help, I believe God's design for us is not to pray as orphans begging Him to do something but as sons and daughters who are confident in His faithfulness that He has solutions for the problems we face. On the other hand I have seen many pray the pain of the problem over a situation: "God, rain down Your fiery judgement over this evil city." When we know mercy's kiss for ourselves, we know how to extend mercy's kiss in our prayers. When we perceive that God is a God of fire and brimstone, our prayers become plagued with the very thing the enemy wants—death and destruction. Notice that verse says, *"We come boldly where love is enthroned."* We receive the answers of His kingdom in His love. His answers are always built on the foundation of love, so why, under

His New Covenant, would His answer for a sinful city be to destroy it? The same principle applies for people. This is why abiding in His presence is the foundation for the solutions of God. We must know His heart; we must be able to receive His love and His mercy in our own lives before we can adequately extend it to others and the world around us. His kingdom is both love and justice, but under the reign of the New Covenant, the cross and resurrection, the covenant of grace, mercy, and redemption, Jesus becomes the kiss of mercy to a dying and hurting world. He invites us to come and sit with Him at His mercy seat, and there we can boldly ask Him the answers that are on His heart for that which grieves Him. It is easy to look at a person, place, or situation through the eyes of judgement, but it is even easier to ask Him, "What do You see?" and partner with His heart, where His mercy triumphs over judgment (see James 2:13). Rather than praying over the problem and begging God for a solution or calling down His judgment, we get to boldly come before Him and have Him share the secret solutions that are stored up in heaven for the problems around us.

This is why in John 15:15 Jesus says, "*I have never called you 'servants,' because a master doesn't confide in his servants, and servants don't always understand what the master is doing. But I call you my most intimate friends, for I reveal to you everything that I've heard from my Father.*" In abiding in the habitation of God, we grow in intimate friendship with Him, and it is in this habitation that His secret solutions for the earth are revealed. When that secret is revealed, He doesn't just show you to give you a piece of information, but He expects you to do something with it. This is where prophetic prayer is released. It is conceived out of intimate love and friendship with the King of all kings and it is birthed into the earth through your love for Him.

As I stood overlooking the sun-glistened city of San Francisco and feeling the grief of His heart, I quietly asked Him, "Father, what are You wanting to do here? What is Your heart for this city and state?" It was a quick moment, a glimpse of a second, because I was holding my wriggling toddler and trying to prevent her inquisitive little eyes and hands from climbing up and over the cascading rock face below us. As I set her back down, out of the corner of my eye I saw the edge of a giant brown wing. I flung around to see what it was, and as I looked up, not ten feet above us were three enormous eagles that had descended upon the area where we were standing. They were circling in perfect unison above the car park and were swooping down, almost as though in a dance, much to the initial delight, turned shock-horror for us and the tourists around us. People began picking up their children, including me, because the sheer size of these birds was both awe-inspiring and terrifying. I kept envisioning my little toddler being picked up in one of their talons and being carried off into the sky above. That might sound like an impossible scenario, but they were evidently hungry and I was not about to find out the likeliness of that imagination. Nate and I quickly made our way to our rental car with both girls in tow, and once they were both locked safely into their car seats with snacks to occupy them, I was able to sit outside the car door for a moment, taking in the beauty and sheer enormity of these eagles.

It didn't immediately strike me that these birds were a prophetic answer to the question I had just asked God. Yet as I took photos, I knew something about this was profound as they continued to circle around and around, just above the Golden Gate Bridge. Sometimes, it felt as though they were close enough to touch, and after about five minutes, two more eagles joined the three. Something felt significant about this. All the tourists at this site were no longer looking out upon the views of San Francisco and the Golden Gate Bridge, but rather, their eyes like mine were to the sky, watching these five eagles encircle us. As we got back in our car and Nate drove us toward Redding, I browsed through the pictures of the eagles that I had just taken. Being from Australia, I wasn't familiar with their species, so I zoomed in and began looking up their identifiable features. As it turns out, they were golden eagles, and I later had them confirmed by multiple sources. When I realized they were golden eagles I recognized the profound, unmistakably prophetic place that we were standing. We were overlooking what is known as "the Golden City," at the Golden Gate Bridge, in the "Golden State" with three and then five golden eagles encircling us. I began to take the pieces of this experience and ask the Holy Spirit what He was saying in response to what I had asked.

IT IS THE GLORY OF KINGS TO SEARCH OUT A MATTER

All too often, we write off moments like this as a natural coincidence. I want to encourage you that as you open the doors wide to the secret place of His presence, to also ask the Holy Spirit to open your eyes to see the miracles and messages within your day-to-day that many, otherwise, miss. God is always speaking. Always. We often think He is silent, but as I have learned, it is in the silence of familiarity where He wants us to discover other ways that He is already speaking to us. The Holy Spirit is fun and adventurous. Jesus said this important statement to His disciples in Matthew 18:3-4:

> *Learn this well: Unless you dramatically change your way of thinking and become teachable, and learn about heaven's kingdom realm with the wide-eyed wonder of a child, you will never be able to enter in. Whoever continually humbles himself to become like this gentle child is the greatest one in heaven's kingdom realm.*

I love that phrase—*"learn about heaven's kingdom realm with the wide-eyed wonder of a child."* This journey of releasing the prophetic solutions of His heart into the earth is not meant to be a boring, serious one, but rather a fun, adventurous discovery of the Father, His purposes, and His ways. Have you ever had to get somewhere quickly with a child in tow? You will know that they don't take the normal route that us boring adults usually do. They stop and find the details. They jump up on the sidewalk, they skip, run, and play to their destination rather than just walking in a stiff, straight line. I could be rushing to load groceries in the car to get back home in time for an important call, and my two daughters will notice the ladybug in the bush next to our parked car and cause me to stop and pause with them for a moment. They see the details of God. They stop and notice. I believe the Father is calling you and me to stop and notice His whispers. Remember the scripture we read in the first chapter:

> *God conceals the revelation of his word*
> *in the hiding place of his glory.*

But the honor of kings is revealed
by how they thoroughly search out
the deeper meaning of all that God says (Proverbs 25:2).

God conceals the revelation of His Word, which is the revelation of Jesus, in the hiding place of His glory. Here we have it confirmed again; the secrets and longings of His heart, the revelation of His answers, all that He is, and all that He has is revealed in the secret place of His presence—His glory, His habitation. When we begin to search out and open our eyes to what He is speaking, it becomes the honor of our life to find and release the answers of His heart into the earth around us.

With these eagles, I began to search out the scripture and found that the eagle can prophetically represent a prophet or one who prophesies the answers of God into a situation. *"You yourselves have seen what I did to Egypt, and how I carried you on eagles' wings and brought you to myself"* (Exod. 19:4 NIV). This verse spoke to me of San Francisco and the Golden State of California, how it has been held in the grips of slavery (referring to the Israelites in slavery in Egypt) under the tyrant rule of the enemy. Next, I researched the Hebrew numbers of three and five, which was the number of eagles that encircled where we were. The number three in scriptures points to the Godhead, completion, perfection, divine fullness, and resurrection. Number five prophetically points to the grace of God, His abundance, His favor, and redemption.

What was God speaking through this encounter? As the eagles encircled, it was a picture to me of His Spirit hovering over the waters of the earth in Genesis 1:2. He was showing me He was hovering over the state of California and the city of San Francisco, waiting on the prophetic word to be released. He is longing to carry them on His wings and bring them unto Himself. Through prophetic prayer, God was going to encircle the two with Himself and bring them into a state of perfection, completion, divine fullness, and resurrection. His heart for California and San Francisco is to pour out His grace in abundance upon their wounds, revealing His favor and bestowing His redemption. This state, this city, was aptly named the Golden State and Golden City for a reason, it is the golden state in His eyes. I believe the California gold rush prophetically declares another gold rush to come—a weightier gold rush of His glory.

PUTTING TOGETHER THE PUZZLES

You may have had similar experiences, or perhaps you haven't yet, but I can guarantee that you will. What I hope to open your eyes to is that through the key of intimacy with God (more on this in Chapter 7) you can unlock spiritual doorways of promise for your life, your family, the culture around you, and your nation. I want to encourage you to get yourself a journal or set aside a section in your phone where you can begin to take daily notes of what you believe God is highlighting to you. Ask yourself some of these questions that may help you to determine the areas God is highlighting that He wants to release His solutions into.

1. What around me needs divine intervention?

Then ask the Holy Spirit this:

2. Holy Spirit, what is Your desired outcome for this problem and what is Your solution to see it restored?

I think the first question can be easily answered. There is always something that needs divine intervention, but what is it specifically that is pulling on your heart? For example, is there increased homelessness in your city that you simply can't ignore? Obviously, I am not suggesting that we are to just pray and then do nothing else. Prayer requires both a natural and a supernatural response. If homelessness happened to be the situation God wanted to use you to release His solutions into, you will likely find that He will release both a supernatural strategy and a natural one into your hands. Both of these strategies may come by the way of dreams, visions, a spoken prophetic word, a stirring in your heart, even a thought. It could also come through a repetitious number that you might see.

Whatever it is that is highlighted to you, it is an invitation to search out more—the glory of kings to search out a matter. I can only give you my own process, which is to search out every little detail. If it is a repetitious number that I see, I will search out the Hebrew meanings of numbers. I will look up scriptures correlating with those numbers. If it is a specific animal that God puts in my path, like the eagle, I will search out its unique characteristics and traits. As though I were working on a puzzle, I begin to put the pieces together—finding the outlines and the corners first and then working my way inward, I finally begin to see a pattern emerge. Prophecy is an invitation of discovery. When you do the same thing, you will begin to see the full picture emerge. Once I see His message coming forward, like I did that day when I discovered the golden eagles at the Golden Gate Bridge, I always then study the scriptures to find that His Word is confirming what I believe He is speaking.

When I know what His solution is, more often than not a strategy is also revealed. Simultaneously as I pray, in some cases a part of the divine solution requires me to physically go to that place and pray over it; sometimes it is to sow a financial seed into a ministry there. Other times, God has required me to actively engage in political processes, while continuing in prayer, to see a situation overturned. One such time was when the Lord instructed me to go and sit in the gallery of our Australian Parliament while they were debating an evil legislation. All I knew to do as a part of this strategy was to go and pray in tongues quietly under my breath as I sat there. As gallery members are not allowed to speak, I prayed silently. As I prayed, unheard by anyone around me, a security guard approached me and with a voice that was not his own, he said to me, "You are disrupting this process. If you don't stop what you are doing, I will have to remove you forcefully." I did not stop praying, because I knew that a demon was manifesting through him and it had no power to do anything; it was a threat.

STEWARDING THE ANSWERS

My sister, Stacey, messaged me recently with a situation she was facing while I have been in the process of writing this chapter, and I knew that what she was sharing was strategic to include in this chapter (with her permission, of course). At the time of writing, she was visiting a rural town in Australia. While there, she immediately noticed that a plague of bats had descended upon the little township. She has been there multiple times before and had noticed the bats before, but this time they had grown beyond plague-like proportions. She sent me a video of the bats flying through the skies at dusk, their swarms so thick that the sky looked black as she drove through the streets. She then told me that it had become so grotesquely plagued that it was even dangerous for them to drive at night as the bats would often fly into windscreens. Some research revealed that the plague had begun two years ago, but in its beginnings it was manageable. City council had since attempted to drive them out and reduce their numbers, but to no avail. Immediately, I knew that this was a problem that required a God solution. I began asking my sister, "What does it feel like there? What do you feel in the atmosphere, aside from your obvious disgust of all the bats? What is it you feel in your spirit?" Her response was simply: "Hopelessness."

I want to give you an insight into stewarding the answers and solutions of God's heart for a region or situation like this. You may be questioning, "Is this just an odd occurrence? Do we really have supernatural authority over what we see in the natural?" Paul gives us some insights into these questions in First Corinthians. He writes, *"However, the spiritual didn't come first. The natural precedes the spiritual"* (1 Cor. 15:46). Paul was writing here about how Adam became a living soul through dust (the natural realm), but the Second Adam, Jesus, became a life-giving Spirit (the spiritual) (see 1 Cor. 15:45). He goes on to say, *"The first one, made from dust, has a race of people just like him, who are also made from dust. The One sent from heaven has a race of heavenly people who are just like him. Once we carried the likeness of the man of dust, but now let us carry the likeness of the Man of heaven"* (1 Cor. 15:48-50). Among the many things this verse is speaking, it tells me that in Christ the natural is now subject to supernatural:

"now let us carry the likeness of the Man of heaven." This reiterates the prayer of Jesus, "on earth as it is in heaven." So when I see a situation like this that is manifesting in the natural, it tells me that it is within our authority to rewrite it from its dying origins under the covenant of the first Adam and speak *life* into it through my covenant with the Second Adam. Simply put, I speak life where there has been death; I plead the Blood of Jesus over the land.

Oftentimes, the natural occurrences like these plagues of bats manifest because of a "natural" agreement. Let me explain what that means. I decided to do some research on this particular township to discover its history and found something interesting.

In its foundation it was a city of gold prospecting. I like to study each and every element when I am searching out an answer, and when I consider what gold represents within the Bible (His glory, refined, pure, and holy—see Isa. 60:9, Heb. 9:4), it tells me that from its very foundations God intended to use this city for His glory. (A book I love to use for this kind of research is called *The Divinity Code* by Adam F. Thompson and Adrian Beale. It gives detailed explanation and scriptural cross references to the seemingly endless prophetic symbolisms within the Bible and in our own daily lives.) So immediately, I see God's intended design for this city was to pour His Spirit into it. His heart for this city, which hasn't changed, is that it would be a city refined, pure, and holy, set apart unto Him.

As I continued to research, I very quickly began to see where God's intended design veered grossly off its path. The boom of gold caused this particular city to grow quickly, and in its rapid growth it gained the enticing nickname, "the world." It became known as a city that people would travel to, with it being said that anything you could possibly desire could be found and had in this city, leaving no reason to travel anywhere ever again. I particularly found that nickname interesting—"the world"—when spoken in light of this warning found in First John 2: *"Don't set the affections of your heart on this world or in loving the things of the world. The love of the Father and the love of the world are incompatible"* (1 John 2:15). I now understood where that natural agreement had been made between men and the enemy of their souls. It also gave insight into why my sister was feeling hopelessness in the atmosphere over that region. The affections of the world are incompatible with the love of the Father, and therefore true hope could not be found.

Upon reading this, I felt led to look up the biblical meaning of a bat, and as soon as I saw it, the puzzle piece was complete. The bat represents idols. In its foundations, the people of this city had idolized the gold instead of the One who created it, they had set their affections on the things of this world. Their natural actions gave way for a spiritual agreement that was made with the enemy, who then was able to keep this township in his grip. Now, I am not suggesting that there are no Christians in this town who don't pray, but what I am saying is I don't believe that particular agreement had been broken with the solution of God. I called my sister and instructed her through the specific solution of what needed to be prayed, saying, "Listen, God may just have sent you there to right this wrong. Though you might feel inadequate, you have the Spirit of the living God on the inside you, and greater is He who is in you than he who is in this world (see 1 John 4:4). Plead the Blood of Jesus over the land and its history, ask the Father to forgive the idolization there, both past and present, then break the agreement with the idolization and decree that the name of Jesus is above every other name. Proclaim that He is King of kings and Lord of lords over this city now. Then, command the bats to leave right now in the name of Jesus. Now, begin to decree God's solution over the city. Begin to prophesy His intention over it that this is a city of God's purity, holiness, and glory, that from there a mighty outpouring of His glory would pour forth and no demon in hell could stop it."

I am pleased to report that within just two weeks of my sister's prayer of authority and declaration, the bats left. In fact, one newspaper headline literally read, "Mass Bat Exodus." I was amazed. The title confirmed what God was longing to do there—set the people free just as He set the Israelites free from their slavery. I informed my sister, "You now have another opportunity before you—to tell them that it was Jesus who moved the bats on." Whether they believe her or not, His prophetic solutions will always create opportunity to bring the lost home. Whether it's San Francisco, a plague of bats, a wayward family member, or an illness, we have the God-given authority to cause His kingdom realm to manifest. We are able to break agreements of the natural and spiritual all because of our new creation in Christ. We are now born of His Spirit, so by Him and through Him you and I have the God-given ability to command every plague of injustice to bow. Then, like an artist, we get to use the paintbrush of His redemption and cover the world with His precious Blood, releasing life, color, and purity wherever we go.

PROPHETIC PRAYER KEY #4

Pray with the Holy Spirit.

The Holy Spirit is always speaking. Have you been seeing signs and clues in your daily life that maybe you hadn't realized were in actuality God speaking to you? What are some of the signs you have been seeing? What are their meanings? What are the solutions and answers they speak into a problem you are seeing? As you begin to write down what the Holy Spirit is revealing to you, search out what He is saying and inviting you to prophesy into.

CHAPTER FIVE

RECEIVING HEAVEN'S BLUEPRINTS

God's designs are far better than our own. In order to release His solutions into the earth, we need to be receiving the designs of our Master Architect. I have often had visions of blueprints, whereby He was releasing His intended design over a matter into my hands. I love this verse that speaks of partnering with His plans:

> *If God's grace doesn't help the builders, they will labor in vain to build a house. If God's mercy doesn't protect the city, all the sentries will circle it in vain. It really is senseless to work so hard from early morning till late at night, toiling to make a living for fear of not having enough. God can provide for his lovers even while they sleep!* (Psalm 127:1-2)

What does this mean for you and me who are His builders in releasing His prophetic solutions? If we do it in our strength, without His grace, we will be laboring in vain. This scripture is essentially telling us that without Him, without His ideas, trying to make something change on our own is senseless work. We need His blueprints and His designs in everything we do. But amazingly, He wants our partnership in the process. In her book *The Happy Intercessor*, Beni Johnson writes:

> In such times, I often *see* faces, places, and situations in my mind's eye. I often feel as if God is showing me things that I need to think about and *brood over* in the way that a mother hen broods over her eggs. Genesis 1:1 says, "Earth was a soup of nothingness, a bottomless emptiness, an inky blackness. God's Spirit brooded like a bird above the watery abyss" (TM). To be honest, most of the time when I am in this place, I just agree. I agree with the plans that God already has for people's lives, for regions, and for the earth. "Yes God, do that, God…go there, Father…that's amazing, Lord Jesus." When I pray this way, I feel as though I am praying from His heart and calling into existence the very desires that are already in the heart of God.
>
> In those times, I feel as though I become the very *womb of God*. "He who believes in Me, as the Scripture said, 'From his innermost being will flow rivers of living water'" (John 7:38 NASB). The words *innermost being* come from the word, *koilia*, which means "womb." We are the womb of God. In our intercessions we are creating and birthing the things of Heaven. We carry the

life of the Kingdom within us (see Luke 17:21). It will flow out of us in our intercessions.[1]

This amazed me when I first read it. I didn't realize I had been praying most of my life from a place of begging God for answers without knowing that He simply desired friendship and partnership with me, and through that He would birth in me the very answers I had been looking for. Our intimacy with God actually impregnates our spirits with the blueprints of His heart for the earth. Without relationship with Him, we are like that builder toiling in vain. Relationship is the key to unlocking blueprints. Many so often ask me, "Why don't I see visions? Why don't I have dreams? How come I don't feel anything? Is there something wrong with me?" Let me tell you about a time in my mid-twenties when the church we were attending was experiencing incredible outpourings of the Holy Spirit. Each and every person in our church was all at once experiencing open-eyed visions and physical manifestations of His presence, including my own husband. I specifically remember one service when a holy fragrance suddenly filled the room. The entire crowd began sniffing the air in awe and amazement as they all proclaimed, "It smells like heaven." However, I sniffed the air and smelled nothing. Absolutely nothing, except for maybe the wafting smell of a dirty diaper in the trash near where I was sitting. I remember feeling so angry and left out. I went home that night and fell onto my bed in a big heap and ugly-cried until my eyes were red. I know you're picturing it right now, and yes, it was the toddler tantrum you are imagining.

When I finally settled down, I heard a gentle whisper, "Will you seek Me just for Me, or do you only want Me for the manifestations of My presence?" His words were gentle, but they shot me straight up out of my bed and out of my self-pity. "I'm so sorry, Father. I want You for You. Even if that means I never experience what others may." That day, I shifted from the mindset of a servant to a friend. I stopped seeking Him for only His outpourings and what He could give me and learned to seek Him for His face alone. A servant begs for food on the table; a servant begs their master to fix all of their problems. A friend talks with their friend about their problems and together they discuss solutions and answers. A friend is moved by the heart of their friend. Likewise, when you are in friendship with Jesus, you are moved according to His heart. A slave is rarely moved by the heart of their master. Your perspective changes from the selfish ambitions of a slave to the laid-down life of a lover. It is the life of seeking His face that unveils the secret blueprints of His heart (see John 15:15).

When my perspective shifted and I sought Him for who He is and His beauty alone, I suddenly began to receive dreams and visions without even working for it. The verse from Psalm 127 began to make sense, where it says that *"God can provide for His lovers even while they sleep"* (Ps. 127:2). Again, to reiterate that point, it says in Psalms, *"Lord, when you said to me, 'Seek my face,' my inner being responded, 'I'm seeking your face with all my heart'"* (Ps. 27:8). Notice that this verse aligns with the verse Beni Johnson shared in her book, John 7:38: *"From his innermost being will flow rivers of living water"* (NASB).

If you want to live the kind of life that Jesus modeled for us to live—a life of power, a life of shifting and transforming nations, a life of releasing His solutions and strategies into the earth—intimacy is the key. For from there flow rivers of living water. It is the lovers of

God who are given the keys to the blueprints written upon His heart. Perhaps you may be saying, "But I do live my life in intimacy with Him, but I'm still not receiving revelation." My answer is this—keep seeking. Don't stop. Continue to seek His face. Keep asking. There is nothing wrong with asking Him for revelation; in fact, He encourages it by telling us to ask and keep on asking, but the key to asking is first found when we seek first His kingdom and His righteousness because then all these other things you have been searching for will be given to you (see Matt. 6:33 NIV)—and your spirit will be able to sustain them and steward them with the heart of the Father in mind. Keep seeking His heart and the answers will come.

INTERPRETING BLUEPRINTS

Perhaps you are one who is already receiving revelations and blueprints, but you don't know what to do with them. Interpreting the blueprints of His heart is simpler than it may seem. I want to give you yet another example of how, in my life, I have learned to interpret and steward God's blueprints and solutions. In late August of 2017, I received a vivid but simple dream. In the dream, I was standing on the steps of the Supreme Court in Washington D.C., and I was holding my Bible open to Psalm 81. As soon as I woke up, I distinctly knew that this dream was about my ongoing calling of prayer to see the end of abortion. This was one of His ideas; this was a blueprint on His heart. I quickly grabbed hold of my nearest Bible and turned to Psalm 81. The words that jumped off the pages at me read:

Go ahead! Blow the jubilee trumpet to begin the feast!
Blow it before every joyous celebration and festival.
For God has given us these seasons of joy,
days that the God of Jacob decreed for us to celebrate and
rejoice.
He has given these feasts to remind us of his triumph over
Egypt,
when he went out to wage war against them.
I heard the message in an unknown tongue as he said to me,
"I have removed your backbreaking burdens
and have freed your hands from the hard labor and toil.
You called out to me in your time of trouble and I rescued
you.
I came down from the realm of the secret place of thunder,
where mysteries hide.
I came down to save you (Psalm 81:3-7).

The title of Psalm 81 as it is written in *The Passion Translation* reads, "For the Feast of Harvest," which is the Jewish Feast of Tabernacles. Knowing that Jewish feasts to this day still hold prophetic significance, I decided to look up when the next Feast of Tabernacles would be and was stunned to find that it was in just five weeks from the date I received the dream. It was due to start on the 6th of October until the 13th of October. I was beginning to understand that a physical response might be required to steward this blueprint.

As I have mentioned in the previous chapter, whenever I am deciphering what the Holy Spirit is speaking through natural means, a dream or a vision, I consider the details. I literally study and pull apart every point of significance that I can find. I write them down until I begin to see a pattern or message emerge. I had shared my dream with my husband, Nate, but had not yet told him about the Feast of Tabernacles. I was getting the sense from the Lord that this was a physical prayer assignment, one that required us to actually travel to Washington D.C., all the way from Australia, with our two small girls. However, the logistics of it all overwhelmed me and I kept thinking, *No, it's impossible. We don't even have the money to pay for four flights, plus accommodation and everything else in between. We haven't even saved for this.*

Yet God wouldn't move from the topic. Two days after I had the dream, Nate called out to me and asked if I had noticed a prayer event that was taking place in D.C. right on the National Mall. It was called "Awaken the Dawn." They were preparing to set up 50 tents on the Mall that would represent the 50 states of America, and it was going to be 24/7 prayer. Amazingly, this event was scheduled to begin on the 6th of October, the first day of the Feast of Tabernacles. Following this event would be another prayer event called "RISE UP" where Lou Engle was calling upon the women of the nation to fast and pray for an entire day for the United States. On the advertisement video, my jaw dropped when they mentioned that they would be praying together to see the end of abortion. My heart exploded. God was orchestrating something much bigger than us, and He was inviting us to play a small part in it. I couldn't believe the parallels between the tents and the "tabernacles." God was preparing to saturate the nation with His living tabernacles, covering every single state of the United States in prayer in one of the most significant locations on the planet.

I began to share with Nate what the Father had showed me in Psalm 81 following my dream, and right at the very moment we were talking we received a text alert that had just come through. Our friend, Torrey Marcel Harper of New York City, sent through a message that read, "Washington D.C. is calling your names." He had absolutely no idea that we were beginning to consider to follow God's call to fly to D.C., let alone the fact that we were talking about it at that exact moment. We booked our tickets the next day and believed by faith that God was calling us, so He would provide what we needed for the rest of the trip.

CRASHING THE COMMUNICATION LINES OF HELL

Have you ever received a blueprint, by way of a dream or a vision or a prophetic word, and you haven't understood what to do with it or what step to take? I want to first encourage you that you will know it is a blueprint from Him if it seems too big for you to carry out. A blueprint is, more than anything else, an invitation into deeper friendship, partnership, and dependency upon Him so that you may work to establish His kingdom together. It will often look different than what you expect. God still, to this day, speaks in a parabolic nature. We uncovered why in the earlier chapters—because it is the glory of kings to seek out a matter. He wants to know we can be trusted with His secrets, so it is only those with a listening ear and an open heart who will find them. Once you find them, it is such a fun adventure to walk them out with Him. I believe that in the coming days of our age, many more of God's sons and daughters are about to be released in covert missions, releasing the prophetic prayers of His heart and ushering in the solutions of heaven into the earth. This is a time of great joy and grand adventure.

Most of the time, however, God will only give you the first part of the mission. He often doesn't fully reveal all that is required until you take that first step of faith into what He is asking of you. I only had one thing I understood to do: Get to D.C. and to the steps of the Supreme Court. I knew I was going there to pray over the 1973 court ruling of Roe v. Wade, and I knew I had to do it the day before the feast began, according to Psalm 81, which said to "blow the trumpet before the feast," which was the 5th of October. I felt like 5:55 PM would be a good time and acted on that with no objection from Him, but that was about all I knew. It seemed kind of foolish in the natural. It wasn't until we landed in Washington D.C. that more would be revealed.

Nate and I, along with our two girls, Charlotte and Sophie, piled into the back of an Uber car, and as we started to head toward our hotel I began to ask the Uber driver some questions. I am constantly fascinated with American politics and I was intrigued to know what it would have been like to be in the city when a recent hostile women's march descended upon the Capitol. Her reply astounded me. She said that when the thousands upon thousands of angry women came into the city all at once, they all happened to be on their phones at the same time. The city could not handle the sudden influx of such a mass using their phones all at once and the communication systems kept crashing. As soon as that was spoken in the car, the Holy Spirit whispered to my heart, "I have sent you here, along with multitudes of my sons and daughters alike, to crash the communication lines of hell over this nation." Prayer is all too often underrated. We don't realize the magnitude and capacity of what prayer can do when we are partnered with the heart of God. I knew then and there that this covert mission was bigger than my mind could comprehend. God will always call you to step into something that is much bigger than what you can fathom or accomplish in your own strength or abilities.

All year leading up to this event, God had been highlighting the numbers "007" to me. This is yet another example of how I see something in repetition and begin to ask the Lord about it: "If You are highlighting this to me, show me what You are saying." In March of 2017, I wrote a prophetic word in response to what the Father was showing me about it. In an excerpt from that word, I wrote:

> Everywhere I go lately, I see the number sequence 007. I am sure if you're like me, those numbers immediately make you think of the Bond movies. I heard the Father say, "I am empowering My intercessors with heavenly insights and unrivalled strength; they are My secret weapons." There was great strength behind His words and He went on to say, "In this time of turbulence, I am commissioning them as My secret agents to destroy the powers of darkness and the enemy's plans. Their intercessions will bring to the light everything that has been hidden in the shadows."

That prophetic word came back to me in the Uber car the very moment I heard in my spirit "crashing the communication lines of hell." I knew then what we were there to do.

MOVING IN YOUR GOD-GIVEN AUTHORITY

When the afternoon of the 5th of October finally came, our family arrived on the steps of the Supreme Court. The unusually hot sun for that time of year was setting and casting long shadows over the tall, majestic pillars that grace the entrance of the magnificent courthouse. I was overcome with the sheer size of this building and, even more so, the enormity of what it represented and what I was there to do in the spirit. I wouldn't have been standing there had it not been for the dream I had received just five weeks earlier, back in Australia. I also wouldn't have been standing there had it not been for the seemingly smaller blueprints God had given me in years gone by. Those smaller designs had allowed me to steward His heart, and now I was stewarding a design that was far bigger than my own capacity or understanding.

I went to the steps and opened up my Bible to Psalm 81 and spoke its words, just as I had dreamed five weeks prior. With Nate standing behind me and our girls running and dancing alongside us, I began to wander around and ask the Father, "Okay, Father, I am here—what now?" I heard His whisper, "Go over to that fountain on your left." As I approached the fountain, I immediately noticed four little statues at the bottom of a flagpole that sat in the middle of the fountain. These four statues resembled in appearance small children or babies and they were holding significant items—a scale and sword, a book, a mask and torch, and a pen and mace. I immediately knew the Holy Spirit was first highlighting this statue to me as a prophetic symbol of His hand of justice upon this issue. I walked back to the steps and found a group of women kneeling and praying

99

and introduced myself to them, only to discover that they were there for the same event we were. God had told them to come to the steps of the Supreme Court at this exact time to pray.

A number of other prayer-warrior friends ended up joining us, and together we laid our hands on the doors of the Supreme Court and decreed that Roe v. Wade would soon be overturned and that justice would prevail for children in the womb and their mothers. My daughter, Charlotte, asked if she could blow the Israeli ram's horn that I had brought with us for this moment, and I felt from God that this was another one of His ideas. She blew it loud. In my spirit I felt a shift, but in the natural it wasn't like angels descended from heaven and the clouds opened up. It just felt very ordinary. We all then hugged and went our separate ways for the night before the event the next day. As we went back to our hotel, a friend of Nate's sent him a simple text. It read, "The Lord just showed me you released something profound tonight. It is significant that tonight is also a rare 'harvest moon.'" When I read that, it prompted my spirit to open up to Psalm 81 again, and in *The Passion Translation*, under the title it reads:

> *For the Pure and Shining One*
>
> *Asaph's poetic song, set to the melody of "For the Feast of Harvest"*

My jaw dropped. *"For the Feast of Harvest."* "What does that possibly mean, Father?" I asked. There is no way I could have orchestrated this in my own understanding. I didn't even know about the harvest moon. As I began to think over the details, I was reminded that it was my daughter Charlotte who asked to blow the shofar, and suddenly the Holy Spirit reminded me of her name's meaning. Her full name is Charlotte Hope. Her first name is derived from Charles, which can mean "free man or warrior." It can also mean "feminine." I could see the picture that God was writing through these details. He caused a little girl to blow the trumpet to signal a time of "harvest" and "feasting" or celebration. A little girl whose name means "free man," "feminine warrior," and "hope" to spiritually signal in a time of hope for the unborn and to rewrite what modern feminism has written into the minds of the earth—that abortion is their right. Am I suggesting that this is the only answer? Not by any means. I am saying that when we follow God's designs, He writes His answers into every detail. I know that we are in the fulfillment of this promise to come to pass, but I know that something significant took place that day and week. God is a God of times and seasons and the way He works is astounding.

He will align events together at just the right moment for a reason. Yet, the effects of prayer that day, along with the prayers of multitudes that would follow in the coming days on the National Mall, would not be revealed until one year later. On the 4th of October 2018, 364 days later, the Supreme Court would become flooded with protestors. Angry demonstrators would flock its outer courts and shout irrationally amongst its pillars. What were they so enraged over? The appointment of a righteous Supreme Court judge. By now, I am sure you can assume the scenario of which I speak. While I don't intend to dig up the details, I will say that it was a demonic witch hunt to destroy the reputation of one man in order to prevent him from taking his position. This was all done by way of the media. Do you remember what I heard the Holy Spirit say to me a year earlier? That the presence of thousands of God's sons and daughters in D.C. that week was to crash the communication lines of hell. We didn't know it then, but those prayers would sit in the heavenly realm like a bowl of incense awaiting the right moment, and they would be poured out a year later (and who knows, they may be continually poured out) and crash the communication lines of hell that would try and prevent the appointment of a righteous judge. At the time of writing this, we don't know it yet, but that judge could very well be instrumental in the future overturning of the abortion ruling of Roe v. Wade.

Your prayers are like covert missions and they are not reserved for some, as I once thought. I once believed the lie that God only gave His blueprints to the elite, but that could not be further from the truth. I am the least qualified to carry out such a mission. It is the heart He is looking for. And as has been the case with me, it is only in the reflecting where I am able to see the magnificent work of His intricate hands all through the details of the blueprint He has given me. You don't need to have it all figured out. All He requires is your love and your willingness to follow Him where He leads. Will you go?

PROPHETIC PRAYER KEY #5

Pray into the blueprints.

Have you received a dream, a vision, or an impression from the Holy Spirit about something that He is calling you to activate? Study it and confirm it through His Word and then begin to write out the blueprint that you see emerging. He may have you physically go somewhere, or it could be a simple prophetic act. Ask Him, and He will show you and confirm it within His Word.

NOTE

1. Johnson, *The Happy Intercessor*, 30-31.

CHAPTER SIX

DISCERNING ATMOSPHERES

One of my earliest training sessions in prophetic prayer was right in the middle of an Indian train station. God often has the tendency of seizing you in prayer in unexpected ways in unexpected moments. Such was the case in the early hours of this November morning in 2008. Nate and I, along with a mission team of about eight, were rushing through one of the busiest train stations in India, Chhatrapati Shivaji Terminus. Flooded with people walking in every direction, the busyness of Chhatrapati reminds me of Penn Station in New York City. A hustling hive of individuals running to and fro, but somehow it felt more frenzied in Chhatrapati, like an organized chaos. We were in India on a missions trip with our friend and his team of roughly five people. We had been traveling together extensively across Mumbai for the past week as our friend, a minister, shared the Gospel through his unique testimony of being born without limbs. Much like all over the world, his story immediately captivates people, but in India his message confronted their cultural views toward those with disabilities. The general belief there is they perceive disability as a curse from the gods. Yet here was a man radiating with a contagious joy and sharing about the goodness of the one true God, Jesus, despite his disability. Needless to say, wherever we went large crowds surrounded him and our team. Our friend had boldly shared the Gospel across television stations, radio stations, in schools, and even in the darkness of the red-light district in Mumbai, and we had seen an amazing response of hunger in the hearts of this nation for Jesus. Now, we were headed with him and the team to a rural region known as Gujarat for an open-field crusade.

Only nights before, the host pastors who were traveling with us had been telling stories of persecuted Christians in Mumbai. They shared horrific events that had recently transpired where traveling ministers had been attacked openly because of their message of Christ. We spent a lot of time praying together, specifically over the coming crusade in Gujarat, which was known to be a difficult region to share the Gospel in. Only six years prior to our visit, the area experienced a genocide aimed mostly at eradicating Christianity, among other religions. Yet in spite of the awareness of the dangers, we all felt a sense of courage and protection. I knew that my role for being there was to surround our friend's mission with prayer. As we raced through the station that morning with our team and over-flowing bags of luggage and camera equipment, it became quickly evident that we were beginning to make a spectacle. There was a heightened sense of awareness in the crowds as we raced through, and we quickly recognized we were the only Westerners in sight with enough baggage and equipment to make it look like we were some kind of international team of journalists.

People were beginning to stop and stare. If you can imagine a scene intriguing enough to halt Penn Station in New York City, we were it. A visible path began to emerge and form around us as we moved through, making it all the more laborious to get to our train with our heavy load of baggage. I cannot remember whether we were running late for our train or if the crowd around us made us all nervous, but in unison we began to hasten all the more. I can still hear the host pastor who was with us as he yelled above the noise of the crowd, "Keep moving, don't stop, keep moving!" Perhaps in this moment, we all began to sense what I was beginning to feel—a spiritual uneasiness. It was a sudden and unmistakable restlessness that began to stir in the very core of my stomach, and it was something I was not familiar with. I began to question myself as we moved through the crowd, wondering if I was just feeling fearful or anxious because of this strange situation we were in. Or was it because of the stories we had heard just nights earlier? Was I overreacting? Being the only female on the team, I also wondered if I was feeling a little unsafe with the number of male eyes in the crowd that seemed to be staring in my direction.

However, what initially just felt like anxiety, I could no longer ignore as it quickly amplified into an alarming sense of terror and the internal urgency increased with every step I took until finally I grabbed my husband's arm. "Nate, I don't know why, but we have to stop and pray." We gathered our team who were gracious to stop in the midst of the mayhem and pray. I did feel like I was acting a little erratic, but I was grateful that they all agreed to stop with me and pray together. As we stood in a circle, surrounded by countless onlookers, all I knew to pray was Psalm 91. It is the psalm that my parents had taught me to memorize when I was only ten years old. I decreed the psalm out loud verse by verse and thanked God for His protection around us. Though I was praying shyly and timidly, as the words from Psalm 91:7 proceeded from my mouth—"Though a thousand may fall at our sides, and ten thousand at our right hands, it shall not come near us"—I felt as though a force or a shield of protection had been released around us. As soon as I finished that simple prayer, an immediate sense of peace returned. In the moment, I did not recognize the supernatural reality of what took place then and there, but looking back now I know that my seemingly simple prayer released an angelic force of protection to surround us. The onlookers did not fade away nor did the spectacle cease as we continued to make our way to the train, but I no longer felt the sense of terror anymore; instead, an overwhelming peace and feeling of protection invaded the atmosphere all around us.

Thankfully, we made our train in time and we went on to do the three-day crusade in the jungles of Gujarat. It was an incredible experience. Over 100,000 men, women, and children, both young and old, traveled on foot, bicycle, or piled into trucks from all over the area through dangerous countryside that is known as tiger and lion habitations. They came with hunger and desperation to hear a message of hope—the message of the Gospel. They were so hungry for this message that they endured a plague-like proportion of insects that accompanied us each night. Literally, the air was so full of the insects that it looked and sounded as though it were raining. Nate was playing the keyboard on stage for worship, and where the floodlights were the insects were in abundance. He was squashing bugs beneath his fingers as he played, and our friend had to have an assigned "bug-swatter" as he preached. Yet each night we witnessed countless numbers responding to Jesus, and one night in particular we all saw a cloud of glory descend upon the crowd. The people began swaying in the visible presence of God in unison and there was a quiet calm as the presence of Jesus settled over them. It was unlike anything I have ever seen or witnessed before. Following the crusade, we traveled back to Mumbai where we remained only two more days and then our team parted ways and headed back home, to both Australia and the United States. It was not until we had just landed back home in Australia that the news broke out.

Nate and I watched in disbelief, awe, and grief as the live scenes flashed across the television. A mass organized terror plot was unfolding in Mumbai. We had barely stepped foot off the plane and begun to unpack our suitcases, yet so much had happened in the short time since our planes had departed. We later calculated that the very moment all of our planes left the ground was the moment that the terrorists began moving in unison across Mumbai. Bombs were detonated in multiple locations. Mass shootings had occurred in cafés, on street corners, and in hotels. There was bloodshed every-where across Mumbai. Terrorists were holding people captive and they were targeting Westerners and anyone else who got in their way; it was as though terror had descended upon the whole city.

What I saw next, though, was particularly difficult to comprehend. The largest shooting occurred at the Chhatrapati Shivaji Terminus where a gunman opened fire on innocent commuters within meters of the exact location where we had stopped to pray just seven days prior. Information began to emerge over the coming week that many of these terrorists had been in Mumbai, watching, waiting, preparing. They had been scouting these exact locations, looking for Westerners. I heard on multiple news reports that the attack was planned for a week earlier, but something had halted their plans. Whether that was legitimate information or not, I knew then why I had an overwhelming sense to pray as we were rushing through Chhatrapati. My spirit perceived a plan of the enemy in the supernatural. It was a prophetic insight from the Holy Spirit to decree protection over our team and partner with heaven to destroy these plots of hell.

I learned an invaluable lesson from this experience. I carried a lot of guilt and shame for many days following this news, wishing that I had identified in the moment to not only pray over our team but to also pray over the entire region. I wondered how different the outcome might have been if I had recognized to pray with a bigger perspective. What if, when I had felt the plans of terror in my spirit, instead of only thinking about our team, what if I prayed over the whole city? I was thankful that I still listened and responded to a degree, because who knows if the terrorists were watching us that day as we rushed through.

I sometimes shudder to think what might have happened if I was not obedient to pray. What if I had written off those feelings as insignificant or an overreaction? Could they have been preparing their attack as we walked through the terminal that day? The words of one news reporter forever rest in my mind: "The terrorists were initially planning their attack one week earlier, but something halted their plans." Could our lives have been cut short? Could the crusade we were headed to have been cancelled, where God was planning to meet and rescue so many of those who were lost? I may never know the answers this side of eternity, but it gives me resolve to pay greater attention to the whisperings of the Holy Spirit when He urges me to pray. That is the very nature of prophecy. To partner with the Holy Spirit and together shift regions, break down demonic principalities, and bring heaven to earth. Not just for us, but for entire cities and nations.

UNDERCOVER AGENTS OF GLORY

We may be living in a time of uncertainty and a time of distraction and confusion, but God is inviting His people beyond space and time into the secret strategy rooms of heaven. He wants to release to you the blueprints of His heart so that you can conquer every impossibility through Him. He is inviting you to be consecrated, set apart, holy, and sanctified so that when you step into an atmosphere that is filled with the plans of the enemy you can immediately discern those plans and destroy them in the spirit. In his book *The Discerner*, James Goll writes:

> Each of us has been equipped with five natural senses: sight, hearing, touch, taste, and smell. (There is also something called "common sense," which some of us seem to lack!)
>
> The first step in beginning to discern God's communications with us entails purposely offering our sense to Him. Unless we do this—on an ongoing basis—we will not be able to grow into the maturity of Christ

Jesus. If we do not give ourselves to Him intentionally, it will be very difficult to know what He wants us to know and therefore difficult to follow Him obediently.

When we surrender our sense to our Creator, He enhances them. Divine input gets "downloaded" less sluggishly than before. As we practice connecting with Him, He increases our capacity for more. What used to seem impossible becomes achievable. I like to say, "One plus God makes the impossible possible." More than that, it is just plain fun! Hearing from God is a perpetual source of pure joy.

Some people call this "activating your senses," and it is that. But you cannot activate your senses on your own; you must activate them by presenting them to the One who created them. You ask Him to anoint them and activate them for His purposes, in love.[1]

I don't know about you, but I want a capacity for more. We are forever students of the kingdom; we don't graduate from learning all there is to know about Him because He is endless. If there is one thing that I have learned with God, there is *always* more. I strongly believe we are entering a time when we are about to see His majesty unveiled in such bizarre and profound ways. God has given you and me keys to His kingdom. That phrase is used a lot in church circles, *keys to the kingdom*, and it is not just a nice term. Keys typically unlock something. They unlock strategies and solutions. They unlock His heart. I believe the Father is speaking to your heart today, wherever you may sit as you read this book: "My son, or My daughter, I have given you keys. What are you going to unlock with them?"

What is behind the doors of His kingdom? We know it is always good. I believe that while the earth may embrace bad news, distraction, and confusion, we get to embrace a higher realm. We have been given the high honor to usher in His secret strategies and solutions. Much like the secret agents of the James Bond movies, only our mission is a mission to assassinate the realm of darkness and open wide the windows of God's glorious light.

Imagine with me for a moment what that might look like in your own life. What if you were driving down a street that you happen to drive through on a regular basis. This particular street passes through a school district and you have driven through it a thousand times before as normal. But suddenly, out of nowhere, you feel an overwhelming unction from the Holy Spirit to pray. You pull your car over, sensing the feeling of terror as I had felt in India, but you recognize it and you disarm the plans of the enemy over that school and that region and you begin to prophetically release warfare angels from heaven. You release the kingdom of heaven over that school and decree that any plan of the enemy to harm this region is disarmed in the name of Jesus. Can you imagine how you would feel if, only a few days later, you discover that the terrorizing plot of a shooter was foiled over that exact school? How would you feel finding out that the local police authorities got an anonymous tip about a particular person who was at that moment preparing their weapons to burst into the very school you had just prayed over? How would you feel knowing that the police had apprehended that person mere seconds before they left their apartment?

What if we take this one step further, where you not only disarm the enemies plans over that region but begin to sense God's prophetic plans for that school and area? After disarming the enemy's plans, you begin to see school meetings erupting in extended praise and worship when it's not even a Christian school. You begin to see young revivalists coming forth from that school, and in the spirit, right there in your car, you begin to call them out. I'm not saying this as a hypothetical possibility, I am telling you this as a definite probability. This is the very nature of releasing the divine solutions of God, and it is what God intends us to pick up and use. He is longing for a people who will set themselves apart in such a way that He is able to engage with us as His undercover agents in every region upon the earth.

SPIRITUAL SENSES THAT ARE AWAKENED TO CHRIST

The writer of Hebrews gives us incredible insight into moving into full maturity in Christ. The first four chapters testify the amazing truths of the Gospel of Jesus. Halfway through chapter five, however, the writer declares that these truths are *"the basics of God's prophetic oracles"* (Heb. 5:12) that are fed to infants, or Christians who are new to the faith. This tells us that there are greater and deeper revelations to be built upon and discovered. In verse 13, the writer, believed to be Paul, writes, *"For every spiritual infant who lives on milk is not yet pierced by the revelation of righteousness."* Interesting. Infants are helpless and need to be fed milk to survive. But those who move beyond the "milk" of the Gospel are then pierced with the revelation of righteousness. Proverbs gives us further insight into what the righteousness of Jesus does: *"Righteousness is like a shield of protection, guarding those who keep their integrity, but sin is the down-fall of the wicked"* (Prov. 13:6). This tells us that those who are pierced with the revelation of righteousness not only carry a shield of protection but *become* a shield of protection to the world around us.

How? Proverbs also tells us in the following chapter, *"A nation is exalted by the righteousness of its people, but sin heaps disgrace upon the land"* (Prov. 14:34). Does this mean that a sin-filled nation is to be destroyed because of its sin? Or is the nation exalted and protected because of those of us who walk in righteousness? The latter is true. When righteousness pierces us, we are able to pierce the darkness around us with the righteousness of Jesus. It becomes a shield of protection to not only our lives and the lives of our family, but to entire nations. The Blood of Jesus redeems sin, awakens the lost to His voice, and rewrites the effects of sin upon the land.

In verse 14 of Hebrews 5, it is written, *"But solid food is for the mature, whose spiritual senses perceive heavenly matters. And they have been adequately trained by what they've experienced to emerge with understanding of the difference between what is truly excellent and what is evil and harmful."* The Greek word used for "senses" here is *aistheterion* (Strong's, G145), which is defined as, the faculty of perception, the organ of sense, and the capacities for spiritual apprehension." The word used for *perceive*, or in other translations *discern*, is the Greek word *diakrisis* (Strong's, G1253), and it means "to distinguish, pass sentence on, decide, and the act of judgment." If we are to consider those definitions in light of our righteousness in Christ, which is the justice of God, and our right standing with Him because of Jesus, you have been given the ability to "perceive" through your "organ of sense" what is good and what is evil and thereby pass sentence upon darkness. In other words, the more you fill yourself with the truth of who you are in Christ, the more it awakens your "organ of sense." This revelation amazes me. Every one of us has been given this gift, and through the Holy Spirit it is awakened as we move into deeper truths where our capacity to discern emerges and we have the authority to pass judgment on the enemy's plans. Whether it is a plan that is in effect or it is something we perceive is coming, God has given you a supernatural organ of perception that is activated upon the revelation of His righteousness.

While this is an amazing revelation, you may be asking, "What does this mean for me? How do I activate this spiritual organ of perception in my own life?" It is likely you are already a believer, and whether new to the faith or old, it is also likely that this "organ of sense" has been activated in your life, whether you may realize it yet or not. At the risk of sounding like a broken record all through-out this book, I cannot stress this enough—the key to receiving and perceiving the solutions of God in your own life is and always will be intimacy with Jesus. Only by and through relationship with Him are we able to move beyond the "milk" of the Gospel and into the deeper truths as Hebrews says. Only in intimacy is the revelation of righteousness revealed.

Trying to receive a solution before the revelation of righteousness is a bit like sending a soldier out onto the battlefield without any for-mer training. While your spiritual senses may already be awakened, without this revelation it will be difficult to perceive *"what is truly excellent and what is evil and harmful."* If you don't believe me, all you have to do is take a look at the world around us that has become consumed by evil. Lies that we once thought were obvious have now become the accepted status quo, and sad to say, many believers too have been consumed by these lies. Why? I can only surmise that according to the Word of God they have not received their own revelation of the righteousness of Jesus, and therefore their eyes are unable to perceive what is good and what is not.

Moving beyond, though, the question still remains, "How do I activate perception in my own life?" My answer is this—simply begin testing it out and ask the Holy Spirit to cause you to be aware of what is going on around you, then speak into it with His hope-filled answers. God solutions always cut through the darkness and release the hope of heaven. When you begin to test this out, you will notice that this spiritual gift of perception is not only true for atmospheres and regions but individual people as well. Recently, I walked into our church auditorium for a Sunday afternoon service at Glory City Church in Brisbane, and immediately I felt an over-whelming sense in my spirit of despair and suicide. I knew that these feelings were not my own but that I was picking up on a spiritual atmosphere from someone within our congregation. It was a feeling I couldn't shake all service. Once our pastor, Katherine Ruonala, had concluded the service, she then asked me and a friend who highly moves in the prophetic, Rebecca Damianopoulos, and a number of other prophetic voices in the house to come to the front and proph-esy with her.

I knew what I needed to do—break the spirit of despair and sui-cide and speak hope over whoever it was that was feeling this way. As I did this, Rebecca came forward immediately after me and said that she had been feeling the exact same thing. She had seen a spirit of heaviness over people, and as she broke it by the name of Jesus in the spirit, something in the room began to shift. As she did this, I then felt the perception of these words in my spirit: "substance abuse," and particularly I could perceive the substance abuse of pills. I then spoke this and broke the chains of addiction and released the hope and life of heaven. Many people stood up and received prayer, and to this day I have received more testimonies from that one night than any other combined. People who were present in the auditorium and those watching the livestreaming online who had been battling thoughts of suicide, depression, anxiety, and substance abuse were set free. I received many online testimonies, particularly in relation to freedom from suicidal thoughts and, you guessed it, addiction to pills. Rebecca later told me that when she walked into the auditorium that night, she physically saw warfare angels lining the room. She said they weren't the usual angels she had so often seen, as she is a seer, but these had evidently come to do warfare. They looked serious and were ready to do battle. We both knew that God had sent those angels ahead of time to await our decrees. The moment we decreed, they went to work.

Likewise, there are angels awaiting your decrees to move and act on what you release. When you feel something, begin to ask the Holy Spirit what it is about. Talk with Him. He knows how to release the solutions of heaven over every problem we will ever face. You may come into contact with a person in your workplace who you perceive the feeling of depression over—just remember, approach it with His grace. It is not meant to be ammunition against the person, but rather, speak the answers of Jesus, speak the hope of heaven over them. The solutions of God are essentially invitations for that person to encounter the goodness of who He is. I truly believe that we are living in a time when we are going to see the Bride of Jesus arise in the splendor of His glory, releasing and orchestrating with Him the solutions of heaven upon the earth. This is not a time to fear but a time to press into His presence and watch Him move. You play a key role in this and I decree over you that this day you shall step into the fullness of your identity and authority as a son or daughter of the King of all kings. God is not subject to this world, but the world is subject to Him—and He is on the inside of you. It's time that He is released in His fullness through you.

PROPHETIC PRAYER KEY #6

Pray with your spiritual senses.

You have been given the authority of Jesus to release His presence into every atmosphere (see Luke 10:19). If ever you feel the presence of darkness, ask the Lord to reveal to you what His plans are for that area and release His solutions there.

NOTE

1. James Goll, *The Discerner* (New Kensington, PA: Whitaker House, 2017), Chapter 1.

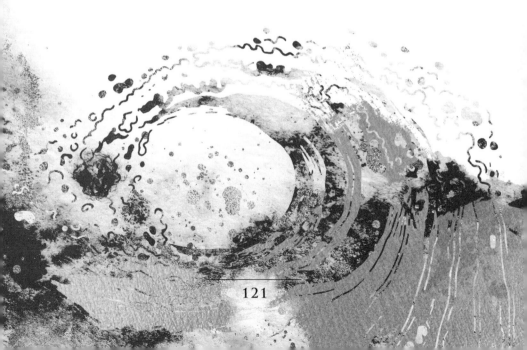

PART THREE

THE GROUNDS OF WAR

CHAPTER SEVEN

WAGING WAR FROM THE MOUNTAINTOP

Who has ever heard of a commanding general sending his troops into a hostile country, in the midst of a terrorist battlefield, without first strategizing a well-designed operation? It would be a foolish general who would not at least first consider the terrain and the enemy which they were dealing with. A wise general would scout out the land, find the weak points of their enemy, and adjust their plan accordingly. They are not going to send their soldiers into a battlefield without first finding out what they're dealing with, what kind of terrain they will be working on, and seeking the counsel of others to orchestrate a plan of attack. The general wants his soldiers to be effective, not slaughtered. This tactic is an important one for the body of Christ. We need to effectively recognize the terrain we are dealing with in this age we have been assigned to. If you are reading this book, it means you are alive and breathing, and therefore you have been appointed to this age of history. When you look around you at the state of the world, you may feel unqualified, but rest assured your Commanding General in heaven specifically assigned you to this territory, He knows the DNA inside of you, He knows you have what it takes, and He has given you the equipment needed to conquer the terrain you have been assigned to. It is important, however, that we understand the terrain we are living in, and by doing so we can prepare and equip ourselves in such a way that we begin to see the fulfillment of our strategic prayers by subjugating the enemy's control over the land we live. •

KNOWING YOUR TERRAIN

You are likely familiar with the terms "the Stone Age," "the Middle Ages," "the Revolutionary Era," or "the Great Depression." The timelines of history have been marked by "ages." They are categorical periods of time that are identifiable by significant events. Each age, like a bookend in time, represents a period in history when notable events transpired and altered the course of that era. The age that you and I are currently living in has been aptly named the "Information Age" or the "Digital Age." Another term that has been loosely coined is the "Age of Distraction," and another I have heard is the "Age of Confusion." I want to pay attention to these two as I believe these terms define the grounds of war that we find ourselves in. If we are to effectively deploy the solutions of God into the earth, we need to know the lay of the land that we are living in. I recently heard Hayley Braun of Bethel Church say in a sermon, *"Your attention is one of the greatest commodities in the world today. There are many people competing for your attention. Instagram itself spends millions of dollars to create algorithms to capture your attention and monetize your interest. God wants your full attention.*" Prophetic prayer is a militant strategy of heaven. God has given this gift to His Church in this hour of history to effectively overthrow and destroy the plans of the enemy. However, the enemy is aware of the potency and power of prophetic prayer, and so he has a cunning scheme at play to dismantle this God-given strategy from the Church through the sly doors of distraction and confusion. It is a crafty plan, one that can easily go unnoticed to those who are unaware. I want to pull back, if you will, the smoke and mirrors of this strategy of diversion to reveal these tactics. It is my utmost prayer that the body of Christ would move into positions of effective prayer, and in order to do so we must approach our enemy's schemes with an even more cunning wisdom than the one he uses against us.

SWITCHED "ON"
TO A HIGHER REALM

Have you ever been in a conversation with a friend or a spouse while they are looking at their phone? It is quite frustrating, if I do say so myself. If you've ever had this experience, you will know that it is not very engaging and almost feels insulting and offensive. It is as though you are competing for their attention, even if what you are sharing is the most amazing, exciting news. When their attention is fixated on the phone, you could announce the Queen of England was arriving and they would probably not even look up from their phones and simply acknowledge your words with, "Oh, that's nice." Why? Their attention is not "switched on" to you, but to the information on their phone. Your words are not absorbed when their attention is elsewhere.

While I don't believe that our phones alone are the problem, they are a perfect example of revealing the tactics of the enemy for this age we are living in. If satan can successfully distract you with a myriad of phone calls, text messages, emails, alerts, notifications, news, dramas, circumstances, and social media feeds all day long, by the end of the day you will be so exhausted that you will have no time or energy to engage with the Spirit of God. It is the subtle deception of this age to be constantly in a state of "switched on" to distraction, effectively wearing down our ability to focus and engage on the higher realm of heaven. If that is the effect that the age of distraction has on the mind, it is easy to recognize how the enemy desires to keep God's people in a place of constant distraction in the Spirit. Whether it's through the means of smartphones, the internet, television, movies, the news, or even through circumstantial drama. As long as he can divert your attention, he can successfully distract you with whirlwinds of drama so that your eyes are constantly fixed on any chaos that surrounds you. If you and I are in a perpetual state of "switched on" to the things of this world, we become like the friend looking at their phone. God is trying to have a conversation with us and share the secrets and divine utterances of His heart, but our eyes, hearts, and minds are fixated elsewhere.

In Second Timothy 3, Paul prophetically describes the characteristics of the last days, and in my humble opinion it sounds very much to me like the days we are living in today. He writes:

> *But you need to be aware that in the final days the culture of society will become extremely fierce and difficult for the*

*people of God. People will be self-centered lovers of them-
selves and obsessed with money. They will boast of great
things as they strut around in their arrogant pride and
mock all that is right. They will ignore their own families. They will be ungrateful and ungodly. They will become
addicted to hateful and malicious slander. Slaves to their
desires, they will be ferocious, belligerent haters of what is
good and right* (2 Timothy 3:1-3).

I wholeheartedly believe that the enemy has used the cunning art
of distraction to create the current mania of deception that covers
the people of the earth like a thick, dark blanket. Those few verses
depict the age of social media, the age of "self," and the age of distraction whereby people have become slaves to their desires and
worldly information. They are malicious with online slander, they
have grown hateful to what is good and right, and they call evil good
and good evil. In verse 7, Paul writes probably the most profound
depiction of today: *"They are always learning but never discover the
revelation-knowledge of truth."*

This age of information has not produced enlightened scholars
of truth but rather confused, angry, and hateful slanderers of what
is pure and holy. In the midst of it all, the enemy's trap is to ensnare
the people of God in distraction with the purpose to draw you away
from the quiet, still, secret place of the King of kings. Satan is more
aware than you know that the secret place is the place of power. It is
the place of God's rest, for it is in the stillness where we find Him.
It is in the stillness where the secrets of His heart are revealed and
prophetic prayer is deployed. I believe we have an invitation before
us, as the Bride of Jesus, to actively enter into the calming place of

His rest by disconnecting from the distractions of this world. I am not suggesting you need to throw your phone away and become a recluse living in the desert all alone, but I am suggesting that we need to instill solid boundaries around everything that would try and steal our attention. Just like the soldier deployed to a foreign nation, you are in a foreign land of distraction, and you must learn to live in it without it affecting who you are and the mission you are called to. It is time we "switch off" from the distractions of this world and "switch on" to the higher realm—the realm of His glory, the realm of His secret place.

ASCEND THE MOUNTAIN

Jesus was the perfect model of intimacy with the Father. He was fully man, yet fully God, and was able to overcome every lie, deception, interference, and temptation. In Hebrews 4:15 it says that, "*He understands humanity, for as a Man, our magnificent King-Priest was tempted in every way just as we are, and conquered sin.*" I am not suggesting that distraction itself is sin; however, it can be a gateway to sin, a pathway for temptation that eventually will lead you away from Christ's higher realities. So, if you and I are to live as Christ did, living in the fullness of His resurrection power and releasing the gift of prophetic prayer with full effectiveness into the earth, we need to know the secret to His ability of overcoming everything that tempted Him, just as it tempts us. I have good news for you—this isn't a five-step program for success. This is a simple, easy, doable key that will unlock for you doors of infinite possibilities. This key will unlock the door of intimacy and it is found in Luke 22:39 where it says, *"Jesus left the upper room with his disciples and, as was his habit, went to the Mount of Olives, his place of secret prayer."*

I want to camp for a moment around that phrase—*as was His habit*. The Greek word used for *habit* in this verse is the word *ethos*. It means "a habit, custom, manner or wont" (Strong's, G1485). It describes one's customary behavior. We can observe throughout the Gospels that it was a commonality for Jesus to ascend a mountain and pray. In Matthew 14:23 it tells us that, *"After the crowds dispersed, Jesus went up into the hills to pray. And as night fell he was there praying alone with God."* Again, in Mark 1:35 it says, *"The next morning, Jesus got up long before daylight, left the house while it was dark, and made his way to a secluded place to give himself to prayer."* Do you see the commonality in these verses? Jesus habitually separated Himself from the people, the crowds, and the distractions and secluded Himself with the Father and gave Himself to prayer. Jesus made it His regular custom to sit and converse with His Father. It was in the secret place where He was strengthened and the Father refreshed Him from all of the opposition He had to face. The secret place of seclusion with the Father was where He received resolve and resolution, strategies and wisdom for the days ahead. You may be asking, "Isn't Jesus God? Why would He have needed resolution, strategies, and wisdom?" He was fully man yet fully God, and He came to model the way of living in the fullness of His power for you and me, as men and women surrendered to God. He came to show us the way of peace and the way of His power. The most effective position we can have is sitting surrendered at His feet.

This is our weapon of offence in the age of confusion and distraction. Sitting with Him enables us to hear His whispers and move in effective authority steps ahead of the enemy, not in reaction to him.

HABITS BECOME HABITATIONS OF GLORY

The Greek word used in the above verse for *habit*, *ethos*, can also mean *character*. When you create the habits in your life to habitually abide in the presence of God, your character becomes more and more like His. Remember, you are the tabernacle of the living God, so as you create simple boundaries around your daily habits you will begin to see how your life is the habitation of God and living gateways. You and I are transformed in His presence—not by striving, not by wanting and trying to change ourselves, but simply by being with Him, He transforms us. It is only in this foundation that the gift of prophetic prayer can be operated in with all of its purity and fullness. Your daily practice of abiding in His presence is the key to deploying prophetic prayer and receiving His solutions for your life and those around you.

> *Who, then, ascends into the presence of the Lord?*
> *And who has the privilege of entering into God's Holy Place?*
> *Those who are clean—whose works and ways are pure,*
> *whose hearts are true and sealed by the truth,*
> *those who never deceive, whose words are sure.*
> *They will receive the Lord's blessing*
> *and righteousness given by the Savior-God.*
> *They will stand before God,*
> *for they seek the pleasure of God's face, the God of Jacob*
> (Psalm 24:3-6).

I believe this scripture is an invitation to you and me in this hour. There is a call that is resounding out from heaven: "Who will come into the presence of the Lord? Who will seek His face? Who will set themselves apart?" If you are alive on the earth at this moment, the invitation is for you. You are one of those who set themselves apart from the distractions of this world and who seek the Spirit of God. The New International Version translates verse three like this: *"who may ascend the mountain of the Lord."* God is calling His people into the mountain of His presence. Remember what God told Moses about the mountain? Mountains in scripture represent the presence of God and simultaneously the high places of the earth. A high place of the earth is a stronghold that is under the dominion of satan. God is calling His children to seek first His face, and by coming into His presence we ascend His mountain and subjugate dominion of the enemy's control over the high places of the earth. The latter part of Psalm 24 says:

> *So wake up, you living gateways!*
> *Lift up your heads, you ageless doors of destiny!*
> *Welcome the King of Glory, for he is about to come through*
> *you* (Psalm 24:7).

Did you notice that word *ageless?* When you make the habit to abide in the habitation of God, you ascend and conquer mountains, regardless of the age we live in. For He has conquered the ages, and when we are hidden in Him, we too are able to conquer the terrain of the age we live in. The age of information and distraction has no power over us, for we have conquered it through the power of the Blood of Jesus. You and I become ageless doors of destiny that are not defined by the age of the hour but release the King of age-less glory into every problem, every situation, and rule over every evil power that tries to inhabit the earth. The Ageless One comes through you when you ascend into His presence—you become His habitation, and you then release His glory into the high places of the earth and the earth becomes inhabited by Him. This is the very essence of prophetic prayer—it is releasing Him into the chaos and His abiding presence turns chaos into order.

WAGING WAR FROM THE SUMMIT OF INTIMACY

In a dream I once had, I was sitting beside a beautiful, rushing river that was sparkling like diamonds. On the other side of the river, just opposite where I was sitting, was a lush and extravagant tree laden with gigantic, ripe, and bursting fruits. Their appearance was like huge, colorful balloons, ready to be eaten as they glistened in the sun. I was so enamored by this tree and all the beauty that surrounded me. Yet there in my hands, I was holding my phone. I was internally torn between the distraction of my phone as it beeped with urgent messages and the magnificence that was all around me. Suddenly, the Father appeared in front of me. Up until that night, I had never dreamed about the Father before, only Jesus. This was unmistakably the Father, in all of His glory and splendor, sitting mere centimeters away, waiting for my attention. He was strength and beauty combined, and not in any way intimidating like I had always thought Him to be. He was welcoming, comforting, and safe. His presence was overwhelming with consuming love, and I could feel His love radiating from His heart into mine as I sat opposite Him. Both of us were sitting on the lush, wispy grass with the flowing river beside us. The dream itself reminds me of Psalm 23:2 where it says, *"He leads me beside peaceful streams"* (NLT). Even though I had experienced breakthrough from depression, this was the first time I had ever felt peace—true, mesmerizing peace.

His face was shining bright and I couldn't quite make out His features because of the brightness that illuminated from Him, but a continual flow of love was oozing and emanating from Him into me. It was like a river of light and love that was cascading from His Spirit directly into mine. He then slowly and gently held out His hand toward me, and immediately I knew I needed to give Him my phone, my distraction. I passed it over to Him and without a moment's hesitation He threw it over His shoulder and into the river beside us. He then leaned toward me as He cupped my face with His gentle hands. The next part of the dream confronted me. He began kissing me all over my face, like a new Father who was beholding his newborn baby. He kissed me on my forehead, my nose, and cheeks. There was such tender affection that it confronted me and I felt myself blushing in the dream, yet it melted me as He held me as His precious child. I felt His adoration for me with each and every kiss. He then got up, and as though in reverence, the tree with fruit that was on the opposite side of the river bent and knelt toward Him so that He could pick a piece of fruit from its branches. The Father then gave me this giant fruit and I took a bite into its bursting goodness. Then I woke up.

I have often been reminded of that dream over the years, and I felt it was a beautiful example to share with you of what it looks like when we focus our gaze and attention onto Him. I feel the interpretation of this dream is quite an obvious one, but I will briefly highlight the prophetic elements of it. The river is a picture of the Holy Spirit and the Word of God. The river is life, love, and death to self, a picture of moving in obedience to His leading and direction. I believe the tree represents both Jesus and the Tree of Life. The tree is a picture of revelation-knowledge—when we are rooted and grafted into Him, fruit grows and wisdom is released. The fruit of wisdom grows from a life that is securely rooted in intimacy and communion with God. The mobile phone is a picture of communication, and in this particular dream it represented the communications of confusion and distraction, looking at and entertaining the lies of this world instead of beholding His face. When we are distracted, it is difficult for us to receive His love and to know our identity as His sons and daughters. It was not until the distraction was thrown into the river that I was able to receive from Him fully and the fruit of wisdom was then given. By simply being with Him in His presence, I was securely reminded of who I am as His daughter. His love washed away all the fears, and by beholding His face I was emptied of all the diversions and fears of this world and filled purely with His love.

This dream reminds me of a beautiful verse within the poetic verses of Song of Songs. Inside of this beautiful portrayal written prophetically by Solomon as a picture of our relationship with Jesus, the Shepherd King (Jesus) is speaking to the Shulamite (a prophetic picture of you and me). The Shulamite had been in her own state of distraction, first with her work, then with her brothers, all of those around her, then even her leaders, her friends, and family. In chapter

4, she comes to the decision that despite all that has been distracting her, she will follow the Shepherd King to the mountaintop (see Song 4:6). He responds to her and speaks of what will happen as they climb the mountain together. He says:

> *Now you are ready, my bride, to come with me as we climb the highest peaks together. Come with me through the archway of trust. We will look down from the crest of the glistening mounts and from the summit of our sublime sanctuary. Together we will wage war in the lion's den and the leopard's lair as they watch nightly for their prey* (Song of Songs 4:8).

I find it mesmerizing that the most effective position for releasing His heart into the earth is where we have ascended the mountain of intimacy and trust. High above the distractions of this natural world, we are positioned to wage war on the enemy. We ascend the mountain of the Lord to conquer the mountains of the earth. What an incredibly beautiful picture of ease and strength. You were never meant to wage spiritual warfare from the ground; it was always meant to be done from the high place of intimacy with Jesus.

The Passion Translation translator, Brian Simmons, writes in the footnotes of the above verse:

> Translated from the Septuagint. The Hebrew is "the crest of Amana." Amana comes from a Hebrew root word from which we get the English word *amen*. This is also one of the Hebrew words for "faith." The crest of Amana is the realm where all God's promises are

kept and realized. Amana can be translated "a place of security."

This is a divine and supernatural place that our spirits enter into with Him, and here the promises of God are kept and realized. How amazing is that? When you enter into this "secret place" with Him, He reveals to you the secrets of His heart, and it is these secrets that are the solutions He holds for the earth. You are given the privilege to then "wage war" with those solutions.

Intimacy with Christ is the mountain in which you wage effective war on the enemy. It is where the secrets and solutions of His heart are heard, realized, and deployed with supernatural power into the earth.

PROPHETIC PRAYER KEY #7

Pray in peace.

Spending time with Jesus in the secret place is an indestructible weapon, one that the enemy cannot penetrate. If you have been feeling distracted and flustered in your prayer life, simply sit with Him at His feet and enjoy His presence. It sounds counterintuitive, but you will be strengthened and refreshed as you do.

CHAPTER EIGHT

THE ASSIGNMENT

There is a scene in the children's movie *Horton Hears a Who* that speaks to me of the power of prophetic prayer. If you haven't seen the movie or read the book, the storyline follows an elephant named Horton who struggles to rescue a microscopic city called "Whoville" from those in his community who do not believe that they exist. The mere idea that a tiny city exists offends his jungle neighbors, and a sour kangaroo works to eradicate the clover on which their city rests. In the final scenes of the movie, the kangaroo manages to retrieve the clover and attempts to throw them into a pot of boiling water. At the instruction of Horton, the inhabitants of the tiny city work together to make a noise, hoping that the kangaroo will hear them. Together, in one accord, they shout, "We are here, we are here, we are here!" With Horton tied down, the kangaroo walks toward the pot of boiling water as Horton shouts to the mayor of Whoville, "Is everyone shouting? You need *everyone!*" At that point, the mayor's son, who had been introverted, quiet, and shy throughout the whole narrative, grabs the horn they had been communicating to Horton with, races to the top of a mountain, and shouts through it at the top of his lungs. This act of bravery breaks the sound barrier mere seconds before the kangaroo was about to drop their speck into the boiling pot. The kangaroo's joey, resting in her pouch, grabs the clover, rescuing them from destruction, and declares, "I can hear them."

I often think of that last scene when I'm in prayer, particularly when I'm praying over something that seems insurmountably large and overwhelming to my natural eyes. I see that little, microscopic son of the mayor, who despite his smallness and timidity shouts into the horn with courage and sees his voice become the cataclysmic force that bursts through the sound barrier. What I love about that scene is it was not him alone that broke the barrier—it was the entire village of Whos rising together in unity and shouting their proclamation. Yet the barrier would not have broken had it not been for that one boy. Had the son of the mayor not been obedient to the call of the moment and stayed silent, that little story, though fictional, would have ended a lot differently.

I see prophetic prayer in much the same way. God needs all of us to be raising our voices, but He specifically needs you. When we pray, we often don't realize that there are multitudes of others whom God has called to pray over the same issue. Your voice, however, is that cataclysmic force that will break through the barriers of hell. Where the prayers of others have contended for many years before them, God is calling His sons and daughters forth to be barrier breakers in this strategic hour of history. While it may seem to you like an immediate answer, it has actually been the culmination of prayers rising from generations past that has caused you to be the catalyst for breaking through.

The earth is in desperate need for the sons and daughters to arise; it is in dire distress, in need of a Savior, and it is your voice that is the force that will break strongholds of darkness over regions. The culminated prayers of God's children rising together in unity will collectively push back the gates of hell over families, regions, cities, and nations. I believe that we as the body of Christ have been thinking too small. We have, in many ways, been focused on our church gatherings and conferences alone, and God is calling us beyond the four walls and into the entire earth. God wants to use you to bring restoration to your family, but He is also thinking much bigger than that. He wants to use you to restore entire nations and generations. You might be thinking, "Me? Little me? How could I help to restore something so big?" As I addressed in the second chapter, insecurities do not define the greatness of our God. When He calls you, He does not consider your smallness, your qualifications, or even your personality—all He requires is your obedience. In fact, the less you have by way of qualifications, the better. It is all the more reason and gives all the more room for Him to be seen through you. I have to admit to you that if I was God (which I think we can all be thankful that I am not), I would certainly not have picked me. I was the least likely person to have courage. I was shy, timid, quiet, and insecure—almost identical to that fictional mayor's son. I love that God doesn't look at our outward appearances or what man thinks is enough.

THE POWER IN THE NAME

When you know your authority in your King, you will walk like David, who marched out onto a battlefield that made thousands of grown soldiers tremble at their knees. What was it that made a young boy, possibly only 15 years old, so brave and so courageous in the face of a powerful and bloodthirsty giant? David didn't see what the rest of the army saw; he wasn't looking with his natural eyes. I believe he saw something completely different. I believe David saw a violation, a direct assault and defiance against God Almighty. We all know the famous story of David and Goliath, but I want to show you a key of your authority found in this story that is often skimmed over and overlooked. We pick up at the beginning of First Samuel:

> *Now the Philistines gathered their forces for war and assembled at Sokoh in Judah. They pitched camp at Ephes Dammim, between Sokoh and Azekah. Saul and the Israelites assembled and camped in the Valley of Elah and drew up their battle line to meet the Philistines. The Philistines occupied one hill and the Israelites another, with the valley between them* (1 Samuel 17:1-3 NIV).

What I want to highlight to you is this phrase, *the Philistines occupied one hill.* It is important to note that the Philistines were occupying a territory that did *not* belong to them. They were in violation of what belonged to the Israelites and they were invading a territory that was not theirs. The land of the Valley of Elah, Sokoh, Ephes Dammim, and Azekah were all the inheritance of the children of the tribe of Judah. David, being a descendent of the tribe of Judah, knew that this land was his inheritance, and there, occupying his inheritance, was an enemy. I believe it was this very thing that caused the courage to arise within him.

I also want to highlight that names are very important in Hebrew history, and I want to uncover the meanings of these territories where this famous battle played out. *Sokoh* means "hedge or fence" (Strong's, H7755). *Ephes Dammim* means "boundary of blood" or "effusion of blood" (Strong's, H658), and *Azekah* means "cultivated ground" (Strong's, H5825). The *Valley of Elah* means "terebinth tree" or "valley of the terebinth" (Strong's, H425). What does all this mean? First, the terebinth tree is a prophetic symbol of encounters with God and His provision. Wherever you see a terebinth tree in the Old Testament, you will find God providing for His people and encountering them under these trees, particularly when they were exhausted. David, being a young Jew raised with godly understanding, would have understood the historical and biblical significance of these geographical locations and names combined.

The Philistines were encamped upon a boundary of blood, symbolic of the sacrificial blood of lambs. This area was known for bloody battles, and as a result it was symbolic of sacrifice where an effusion of blood had been poured forth for the Israelites' freedom. This was a ground that had been cultivated with precious blood, and it was a hedge or fence of protection over the people of Israel. It was also symbolic of a valley of provision and encounter with God. David, although young, understood that the Philistines did not belong on this sacred ground and a righteous anger arose within him to destroy them before they destroyed what rightfully belonged to the Israelites. He saw the violation and arose to overturn it.

When David faced Goliath, he shouted to him the answer, *"You come against me with sword and spear and javelin, but I come against you in the name of the Lord Almighty, the God of the armies of Israel, whom you have defied"* (1 Samuel 17:45 NIV). Isn't it amazing that when the enemy defies you, he is actually defying God?! When he tries to occupy a land that has been given into the hands of God's children, he is defying the Lord Almighty Himself. All it takes is one son or daughter to stand up and decree as David did, *"I come against you in the name of the Lord Almighty."* This is the calling of releasing prophetic prayer into the earth. It is not on our dependence, but in His name that we find our victory. I love that in the next verse David prophesied the giant's defeat in front of the eyes and ears of Israel's armies and the Philistine armies before it even happened. What is stopping you from prophesying victory to your life and those around you? David called forth the end result, saying:

> *This day the Lord will deliver you into my hands, and I'll strike you down and cut off your head. This very day I will give the carcasses of the Philistine army to the birds and the wild animals, and the whole world will know that there is a God in Israel* (1 Samuel 17:46 NIV).

The Father is looking for a people upon the earth in this moment of history to see the violations of the enemy and call forth his defeat. Prophetic prayer is not merely praying over our problems, but calling out the end result of victory in His name. The name *Goliath* means "to uncover, remove, or go into exile" (Strong's, H1555). This meaning exposes the plans of the enemy himself—to uncover the promises of God, remove them, and cause God's people to go into exile. An uncovered people are an unprotected people. But the name of Jesus covers every violation he sends against us. The victory that David found was not in his stones or his sling; it was in the name he ran toward the giant with. He said *in the name of the Lord*, which translated there is Yahweh—YHWH. It was the name that infused David's arms as he swung that sling, it was the name that brought keen precision to his eyes and his hands as the slingshot released the stone, it was the name that carried that stone directly to the forehead of the giant. It was the name of the Lord, Yahweh, that slammed that enemy giant into the dust of the ground.

When David cut off the head of the giant with Goliath's sword, scripture tells us that he brought the head to the city of Jerusalem and buried it there, outside of the gates, as was custom. If we look forward to the time of Jesus when He was crucified upon the cross, we see that He was crucified in a place called *Golgotha*, or "The Place of the Skull." That word *Golgotha* is derived from "Gath," or as we know him, Goliath of Gath (Strong's, G1116). Many scholars believe that Jesus was indeed crucified upon the place where Goliath's head was buried. Not only is it a prophetic picture of Jesus' Blood covering all that has been uncovered within us, it powerfully points to the authority we now have in Christ. Everything that the enemy tries to uncover or remove can be lawfully covered by His Blood and redeemed upon the authority of His mighty name. The name *Goliath* can also mean "exposer or rapist." This horrifying definition tells us that the enemy is the one who seeks to defile the promises of God, but Jesus destroyed that power and authority satan once had by dying in our place. His Blood covered and crushed the head of the exposer. It is by Jesus' name that we deploy His solutions into the earth, exposing all of the places that the enemy tries to occupy, and call back into alignment what rightfully belongs to us. This is our assignment—to see a violation and run toward it with the name of Jesus.

> *Because of that obedience, God exalted him and multiplied his greatness! He has now been given the greatest of all names! The authority of the name of Jesus causes every knee to bow in reverence! Everything and everyone will one day submit to this name—in the heavenly realm, in the earthly realm, and in the demonic realm. And every tongue will proclaim in every language: "Jesus Christ is Lord Yahweh," bringing glory and honor to God, his Father!* (Philippians 2:9-11)

YOU HAVE THE POWER OF ATTORNEY

Did you know that you have the same ability to perceive a violation and then overthrow the enemy, just as David did? You have been given the power of attorney. In legal terms, the power of attorney is a legalized document where a person gives another trusted person the legal authority to move and act on their behalf. The power of attorney is in the document; it is the signed authorization for this person to move in the same power of authority as the signee. Whatever the signee owns is legally given by way of managing their affairs. Let's paint the picture, for example, that you are the owner of multiple wealthy golf course estates. Your golf courses are found in every state of your country. They are well-renowned courses and are known to increase the economy of the cities that they are in simply because of your name upon the estate. You have given your life to the upkeep and increase of these estates, but you feel it is time to rest—not retire, but to spend some quality time with your family who live in a foreign country for a season. You may be gone for months on end. In your absence, you will need someone you can trust to manage the affairs of your courses. You would want to choose an advisor whom you could trust, someone who had worked with you, who knew the cost of your labors and knew your heart. You would want someone who knew how to respond the way that you would to a matter or a crisis and would act on your behalf. This is what the power of attorney does—it entrusts the *full* authority of your affairs, upon the basis of your name, to the entrusted person. This is what has been given to us—the kingdom of heaven upon the foundation of His powerful name. When we gave our lives to Jesus, we were sealed in an agreement of heaven, by the Blood of the Lamb and the word of our testimony, and given full power of attorney over the earth. It is clearly written in John 14:12-14:

> *I tell you this timeless truth: The person who follows me in faith, believing in me, will do the same mighty miracles that I do—even greater miracles than these because I go to be with my Father! For I will do whatever you ask me to do when you ask me in my name. And that is how the Son will show what the Father is really like and bring glory to him. Ask me anything in my name, and I will do it for you!*

You have been authorized to act on His behalf. You have been given the power of attorney to manage His affairs on the earth. So when you see a violation, it means you have His full authority and backing to prophetically decree the solution of God over that violation and rewrite every wrong. Jesus, the second Adam, came that we might fulfill the original mandate of the first Adam, which was in Genesis 1:28: *"And God blessed them, and God said unto them, Be fruitful, and multiply, and replenish the earth, and subdue it: and have dominion over the fish of the sea, and over the fowl of the air, and over every living thing that moveth upon the earth"* (KJV). Your power of attorney, in the name of Jesus, is to fulfill this mandate—replenish the earth and subdue it. The Garden of Eden was supposed to extend to the four corners of the earth, not be barricaded in. Now, in His name and upon His authority, He has given us the commission to *"go into all the world, preach openly the wonderful news of the gospel to the entire human race!"* (Mark 16:15). Amazingly, the name *Eden* means "delight." Jesus came to restore His delight upon the earth. Pressed and crushed in the Garden of Gethsemane, He rose in the Garden tomb that the Garden of Eden might be restored—in you and through you. You have now become His delight, and in your voice is the authority of His name to multiply His delight, replenishing the earth through your prophetic prayers everywhere you go.

MESSIAH'S MISSION

You might be asking, "How can I detect a violation? And once I do see one, how exactly do I use my authority to overturn it?" Easy. A violation is anything that stands in defiance of its original design in God. How can you discern the enemy's rebellion over a person or region, though? I want to show you an example. My grandfather was a devout atheist. I vividly remember him mocking my dad at any mention of the name of Jesus. His spirit was in captivity to the lies of the enemy. This was not God's design for him. God has designed every human being with the need for Him, so when a person defiantly objects and even mocks God, we can easily recognize it's not the person but the enemy at work behind them, defying God through their thoughts and beliefs. I watched my dad struggle for many years with his father, praying for his salvation. I remember him often calling his father out in prophetic prayer saying, "Ray, you will come to know Jesus. In Jesus' name, you will be saved!" My dad, Terry, saw the violation and called forth the prophetic answer on the authority of Jesus' name, though it looked impossible in the natural. Many people give up on their prophecies because they don't see immediate results, but I want to encourage you—it is persistence in faith and persistence in decreeing the solution ahead of time that will prevail (more on that in later chapters). When my grandfather suddenly died, our family went into shock.

My father experienced immense sadness beyond normal grief, though, as one of the last conversations he had with his father before he died was again how he did not believe in God. I was 17 at the time and something within me just knew. I had this sense of peace that my grandfather had somehow given his life to Jesus in his final moments. I had a dream one night, not long after his death, where he was walking the streets of gold and shouting in awe and amazement, "Terry was right! Terry was right! Jesus is real!" At his funeral, that dream was confirmed when a beautiful indigenous woman of our congregation, who is also now with the Lord, revealed something that none of us knew. She shared with tears streaming down her face that she had talked with my grandfather just one week before he had died. A conviction had arrested his heart and he was secretively questioning her about Jesus. As she shared with him the wonderful Gospel, she asked him if he would like to receive Jesus in his heart, to which he said yes. Right there, near the steps where his coffin lay in front of us, just one week prior he had given his life to Jesus. She finished by saying, "Ray explicitly made me promise never to tell Terry as long as he lived, but I figured that promise no longer stands." To which we all laughed. My grandfather was a stubborn man, but we all witnessed there that day the fulfillment of the prophetic promise and the prayers my dad had prayed.

It's easy to detect a violation once you know the original design. Another example is where I have received multiple dreams and visions over Hollywood. I have had dreams where I saw a tidal wave of God's glory cleansing and purifying the filth that has come out of the entertainment industry. Recently when we were in Los Angeles, my daughters wanted to see the Hollywood sign that they had seen on a handful of children's movies. When we took them in there, my youngest daughter kept correcting me. Every time I said "Hollywood," she would say, "No, Mum, it's *Holy*-wood!" She had never heard me or anyone else ever say this before, but I recognized that it was her spirit perceiving God's intended design for the arts, and she was automatically prophesying the solution. Likewise, when you are in tune with God's original design, you can be driving past an area of your neighborhood, and suddenly the Spirit of the Lord will come upon you and divinely reveal to you that there are violations of drugs happening in the homes you may be driving past. The Gospel wasn't designed for the four walls of churches alone; it was designed for the world. He came for the lost, and His authority is in the hands of His Bride to reset the foundations according to His design. We do so by decreeing His solutions. You may only have to decree those solutions once or twice, or maybe you will need to do it a thousand times over—the key is in the persistence. We do not move from His prophetic solutions until we see them manifested. We keep striking that rock of stubborn resistance, just as my dad had to do with his father—he had to prophetically strike the stubborn resistance within him. The answer, though it tarried, was fulfilled. It is your inheritance to inherit His kingdom. Don't do nothing with it; it's time to pick up your rod of iron, which is your authority in Christ, and strike it. Increase your vision, son or daughter, increase your capacity to believe that God has given you His rod of authority to smash in pieces every violation that the enemy would try and raise up in defiance against Him. It is time to take back the territory and inheritance that belongs to you.

In Psalm 2:8-9 is a mantle of prophetic prayer, saying:

> *Ask me to give you the nations and I will do it, and they shall become your legacy.*
> *Your domain will stretch to the ends of the earth.*
> *And you will shepherd them with unlimited authority, crushing their rebellion as an iron rod smashes jars of clay!*

PROPHETIC SOLUTION KEY #8

Pray with the Name of Jesus.

Know your assignment by discerning the enemy's violations. What violation of the enemy do you yearn to see restored back to its original God-design? It could be an area of injustice like abortion or human trafficking, or perhaps you feel a calling to release purity in the entertainment industry, media, or teaching. Ask yourself also— where is the enemy illegally occupying in your life, a member of your family, or in your nation that is a blatant and direct violation of God's intended design for you or them? Ask the Lord for His promise over that violation—what is the prophetic solution of His heart? Begin to prophesy the answer as though it has already manifested.

CHAPTER NINE

HIDDEN TRAPS

A s I was praying over this particular chapter before writing it, the Holy Spirit kept bringing a term to my heart. I kept hearing "IED." In case you're not familiar with it, it is a military term short for "Improvised Explosive Devices." I found the following definition of what an IED actually is to be especially eye-opening for what you are about to read in this particular chapter: "An IED is characterized as a low-technology exploding mine, usually 'homemade,' that is often hidden beside a roadway and set off using a variety of trigger mechanisms."[1] IED's are sadly accountable for more than 2,000 deaths and casualties in the U.S. coalition forces alone. What stood out to me in that definition though is that IEDs are described as "low technology." How can something that is so basic be so destructive?

I began to ask the Holy Spirit, "Why are You showing me this for this chapter?" Immediately, I felt His voice impress upon my heart, "The enemy works in the same way with My children. I want you to expose his hidden traps. His devices are basic, but if you are unaware of his cleverly disguised motives he can easily trigger you, which will ultimately be explosive to your deployment of prophetic prayer and destiny combined." How many of God's sons and daughters have been taken out of their assignments because of an IED hidden beside the roadway of their life? The question, then, is how do we identify these IEDs and disarm them before they have a chance to explode? What do we do if they do explode? I want to show you through the experience of my own personal journey what I believe is the enemy's number-one formula in destroying prophetic prayer and aborting the solutions of God in their tracks.

WEIGHED DOWN AND INEFFECTIVE

My call to prayer began at a young age, though I didn't know it then. One of my earliest memories of this call was when I was just eleven years old. A very well-known celebrity was touring Australia with his latest musical release. It was all over the news and in every newspaper. However, I remember feeling a heavy sense of grief whenever I heard anyone talk about him, and finally one night as my mum was praying for my siblings and me before bed, I broke down in tears to her as I told her how sad I was feeling for this celebrity. I don't think she even fully understood what brought on this emotional outburst of mine, but what she prompted me to do next helped to teach me how to pray in the years to come. As she asked me questions, it came out of my spirit that I was grieving for this man to know Jesus. So, she prayed with me for him and I felt a release and was able to fall asleep in peace. I remember her saying to me, "Whenever you feel sad for someone, pray for them rather than carrying the sadness around." I'll never know the effects of those prayers until heaven, but all I know is, when you are faithful to pray, God moves. I didn't know it was prophetic prayer then, nor did I know that I was called to pray and intercede, but as I grew into my adult years those feelings often grew stronger. I want to make clear that God never puts "heaviness" on a person, but I do believe that He will use our emotions, if they are in check with His Spirit as we discovered in Chapter Six, to reveal certain prayer assignments. Some call it "a burden in prayer." For me, I believe it is less of a burden and more of "a prayer assignment." However, therein lies what I believe to be one of the enemy's most effective IEDs to prophetic prayer.

Have you ever seen an intercessor, someone who is not just called to pray like every believer, but someone who operates in the gift of intercession, yet they always look heavy, downcast, and depressed? I don't believe this is a sign of spiritual authority but, rather, not knowing how to handle the assignment properly. I believe this is a sign that the assignment has become an oppressive burden rather than a joy. Our assignment in prayer is not meant to be a depressing one but a joyful, fun, adventurous one. Yes, it involves a labor of sorts, but I do not believe that the labor was designed by God to be a horrible, tedious one. It's a partnership with Him, and it requires constant dialogue with Him. This is where I have noticed that many prayer assignments fall apart. If you don't recognize the tension you are feeling in the spirit, or perhaps seeing in dreams and visions, you will either perceive it in one of two ways, which are the IEDs of the enemy. The first way is thinking that the answer to the problem rests solely on your shoulders.

When I first began walking in prophetic prayer, I came under this very weight of dark heaviness. Particularly when God released one of my specific prayer assignments to pray to see the end of abortion. What started out as an assignment very quickly turned into a heavy burden, and not because God wanted it that way but because I lacked the understanding of how to operate effectively in this calling.

I remember feeling emotions of frustration and anger that it seemed "everybody else in the world wasn't seeing what I was seeing," which I know now to be untrue. The reality is God calls many to pray over a certain situation, but the enemy will try and deceive you that you are all alone in the matter.

I also remember feeling the urgency to pray and perceived that these unborn children were dying on a daily basis as a result of my inability to pray enough or effectively enough. "Perhaps I need to spend more time in prayer, get up earlier, go to bed later?" I was also a full-time, stay-at-home mother to a one-year-old and a three-year-old and some days I felt like I was in a tug of war between what I was called to do in the natural as a mother and what I was called to do in the supernatural in the spirit. I had days when I felt like I wasn't doing enough, praying enough, *being* enough. I was never able to measure up to what I thought was God's standard in prayer, and I constantly felt as though I was walking around with the weight of the world on my shoulders. When I felt like this, I was less inclined to pray. Or, when I did pray, I wouldn't pray prayers of faith and prophecy, but I would pray from a place of begging God to move. Begging God to move is not faith. Prophesying His answers, on the other hand, is. The enemy had caused the very assignment I was given in prayer to become a heavy and weighty burden that eventually dismantled the designed purpose of my calling in the first place.

I remember crying out to God one day, "Why did You give me this burden? I can't carry it anymore, it's too heavy and enormous." I'll never forget His simple but telling response to my heart, "I never asked you to carry a burden." His answer made me angry. "Yes, You did! You gave me this assignment to pray to see the end of abortion. I can't do it. It's too much for me. I feel guilty that nothing is happening quickly enough and then I feel frustrated that I'm all alone." His reply has stayed with me all these years: "Who told you that you were alone? Who made you to feel guilty and frustrated? Because it wasn't Me."

My mouth hit the floor and my body quickly followed as I asked for His forgiveness. All this time, I thought that a part of my prayer assignment was to feel forlorn, cast down, and weighed down by it, but all along He was simply desiring me to partner with Him and prophesy into it. He then began to teach me how simple and effective prayer and prophecy can be. He also began teaching me how my first assignment was to minister to His heart. I barely had a spare second in my day as a mother of two young children, but I began to daily ascend the mountain with Him and fill my home with worship. I realized that my first ministry was to Him and to my family, and from there—right as I would be preparing food for my two little daughters, or doing the washing, or putting away dishes—He would suddenly impress something on my heart to pray. He began to teach me in the day to day, step by step, the power, authority, and joyous simplicity of prophetic prayer. I would speak and declare what He showed me and then simply move on, without the ongoing weight of what I had previously carried. Prayer became less and less of a burden and more and more of a dance with Him. He would move this way, and I would follow Him; He would move that way, and I would follow His lead there too.

The enemy wants to dismantle the power of your prophetic prayers by detonating them before they have a chance to leave your mouth. The first IED he uses is this very crafty but simple one—to weigh you down with the burden of the assignment, to make you feel that the weight of the answer is all on your shoulders, that you are surrounded with ongoing onslaught, and that you are destined to live your life treading in stormy waters, just barely keeping your head above water. It sounds too simple, doesn't it? That's why it's an IED—it is his homemade weapon crafted out of the same tactics he has used from the beginning of time with Adam and Eve. First he isolates you, then he causes you to question the assignment, and finally, at the heart of his tactics, he causes you to question the power and ability of God. When you are walking around with a cumbersome burden in prayer, you are not moved by faith but doubt. This is why, I believe, many abandon their assignments of prophetic prayer in the first place. Far too many have come to believe this crafty deception of the enemy and run in the opposite direction of their calling for fear of becoming a depressed intercessor. I believe the Holy Spirit is wanting to give you and me an upgrade in our language and understanding surrounding prayer so that we are aware of these hidden IEDs of the enemy that are designed to weigh us down and detonate prayer in its tracks.

I consider myself an ongoing student of the Word, so I am always looking for ways to learn more. On a recent trip into Los Angeles, this same IED I am writing about caught me off guard. The moment our plane touched down, I felt suddenly aware of the principalities over the region. There's no explaining it if you have never felt this before, except that you can sense the tyrant demonic forces that inhabit that area, and let me just say—it can feel tormenting. If you aren't familiar with it, you'll likely internalize it. I knew what it was, but I also knew I needed some backup prayer. A powerful friend by the name of Jenna Winston, whom we had just become acquainted with, randomly reached out to Nate and told him that the Lord had put me on her heart and that she needed to come around and pray over me. I was relieved. As soon as she arrived, I began blurting out everything that I was feeling. (In hindsight, I should have reread this chapter to myself.) She stopped me in my tracks and said this: "I am going to teach you a prayer that is going to change your life." She then had me repeat and pray this simple prayer: "Jesus, I cast off any weight that is not my own to carry. Make me more aware of what You are doing in the atmosphere than what I can feel the enemy is doing." That simple but effective prayer shifted the atmosphere immediately.

LIKE A LION

In First Peter 5:8, we are given a very insightful illustration into the enemy's tactics, which teaches us how to be alert in our assignment of prophetic prayer and be aware of these IEDs. It says, *"Be well balanced and always alert, because your enemy, the devil, roams around incessantly, like a roaring lion looking for its prey to devour."* If you have ever watched a National Geographic show about lions, and if you're anything like me, you will have squirmed in discomfort as you watch the unsuspecting gazelle drinking from a watering hole with a lion stalking in the grass, mere meters behind her. Have you ever noticed the lion doesn't hunt as much when the gazelle is alert, well-rested, and full of energy? Why? When the gazelle is alert, she sees the lion coming from afar off and is prompted to escape faster and run more quickly. When she is in a state of awareness, it wears down the lion's ability to stay in the fight for its food. However, when the gazelle is in a moment of weakness—usually when she is foraging for food, drinking from the waterhole, resting, or even giving birth—she is in a state of vulnerability and weakness. When she is vulnerable, it is much easier for the lion to capture her and lock her in its jaws. Notice that verse tells us to *"be well balanced and always alert."* We aren't meant to ignore the enemy's tactics, but to be alert to them while staying intently focused on our goal of deploying the strategies of God into the earth.

Another point I want to highlight about that verse is this—the enemy is *like* a lion, but he is *not* one. God is showing us a very clear depiction here. There is only *one* lion, and that lion is the Lion of the Tribe of Judah. We are the offspring of the true Lion, but we are to be aware that the enemy always mimics; satan wants to be like God, so everything he does is always in a mimicking response to God's higher ways. So, what does it say about you and me then? It means that Christ is the Lion who hunts His prey, every demonic principality and deception, with unsuspected precision. How does He do it? His roar is released through you with the power of prophetic prayer. Prophetic prayer is like a shock factor to the enemy. He doesn't see it coming, he doesn't suspect it, and suddenly the jaws of the Almighty Lion of the Tribe of Judah are around his neck, rendering him helpless. When you are alert, as Peter tells us, you are not vulnerable to the enemy fake lion, but rather are empowered to operate in the authority of the true Lion.

How does this false lion manage to capture so many with his hidden IEDs though? When it comes to the release of prophetic prayer, I believe satan's number-one tactic is to cause you and me to become so overwhelmed with the negative weight of our friends, families, and the world's problems that we are eventually rendered useless. I believe that there is the gift of empathy and compassion within the calling of prophetic prayer, but the enemy will often tweak this gift and turn it against us. Where we see God's heart for a matter and are moved by His love and compassion to see that shift according to His purpose and plan, sometimes the assignment in prayer does not bring an overnight answer. When there is a stubborn resistance, like in the case of abortion, it can become very easy to see despair, and we begin thinking we are not praying effectively and get weighed down as a result. I want to give you a spiritual key that will unlock the door to remaining effective in prayer, and by doing so you will disarm this very crafty IED and counterattack the illusionist lion at his own game.

CASTING YOUR CARES

Right before Peter speaks about this crafty, illusionist lion, he delivers a key for overcoming his tactics. In First Peter 5:7, he writes, *"Pour out all your worries and stress upon him and leave them there, for he always tenderly cares for you."* As we will talk more about in a moment, the assignment of prayer is not meant to be something that you carry around as a heavy, depressing weight. While there is an element where you are moved by empathy in prayer, if that empathy turns into a cumbersome suffering of sorts, you can be assured that an IED has been detonated in your domain of prophetic prayer. You will need to acclimatize yourself to God's perspective again and ascend back up on the mountain in intimacy with Him once more. The New International Version translation for this verse simply says, *"Cast all your anxiety on him because he cares for you."* That word *cast* means "to throw off violently." I remember sharing this verse with my grandmother when she was facing a problem in her life, and she said to me, "Oh wow, that reminds me of 'cast' sheep."

I had never heard that phrase before, and so she began to tell me the story of when she used to look after a friend's farm in the green foothills of Napier, New Zealand. Right before the spring shearing time for the sheep, the weight of a sheep's winter wool would weigh down on it so heavily that it would sometimes fall over. When a sheep laden with winter wool had fallen over, it was termed as "cast." So every morning and afternoon, she would have to look in the fields for cast sheep. It is a life-or-death situation for a cast sheep as they are unable to get back up because their center of gravity is off and gases begin to build up in their abdomen and they can die within hours.

When I looked this up on YouTube, I discovered a video of a shepherd detailing how to take care of a cast sheep. He gently helped the sheep back up onto its feet, and then, with his hands on both sides of the sheep's head, he held it in place and spoke softly to it until it regained its composure. The sheep was then able to run off as normal again. This resonates with me for prophetic prayer. When we are weighed down unnecessarily by "burdens" in prayer, we are like that cast sheep that falls over and cannot get back up. We need to violently throw off the weight of that wool and give it to Jesus. When we give Him the weight of prayer and prophesy to the situation, He carries the burden for us. But when we do find ourselves cast down like the sheep or taken out by an IED, all we need to do is to call on Him. Just like the Good Shepherd that He is, He will speak gently to us with His firm hands cupped around our faces and recalibrate our mission in prayer so we can effectively release His strategies and solutions into the earth.

THE TRUE BURDEN OF PRAYER

You might be wondering, "Isn't the 'burden of prayer' actually mentioned in the Bible though?" The answer is yes, but not as you may think. The term *burden in prayer* has become a popular one and I hear it often, but there is a misconception in it. Whenever I have heard this term coined, it has more often than not been to describe a burdensome, weary, heavy load and task of prayer from the Lord. So for that reason, I want to clear something up. In my studies of the scriptures, I could find many verses that reference the word *burden*. However, concerning prayer I could only find a handful, and I want to show you something amazing. The English language is very limited and one-sided; however, in the Bible's original translations of Hebrew and Greek, words have multiple meanings and layers of depth. For us English speakers, it means that we must dig into the original translations and meanings to discover what is really being said. Perplexed by this terminology of *burden in prayer*, I began to ask the Holy Spirit, "Why would Jesus say in Matthew 11:30 that

His yoke is easy and His burden is light, but then in Galatians 6:2 it says we are to bear one another's burdens?"

Because I don't know about you, but bearing someone else's burdens on top of my own sounds like a heavy task to me. I only have to assume that many people feel the same way, because any time you mention a bigger problem in the world, it's almost too much for most people to handle. I used to work as office administrator in an office that had a prayer-call ministry, and while I loved working there it was this one particular department that I used to dread being drafted into. Whenever the staff whose jobs were to take prayer calls all day were on their lunch break, the rest of us were on a roster of taking those calls, and each and every week I dreaded my turn. On one hand, I loved to pray and this was a great training ground in prayer for me, but on the other hand, as a twenty-two-year-old, I found people's prayer requests, problems, and situations to be overwhelming and burdensome.

Think of it like this—imagine spending an entire hour just hearing about strangers' problems. It was pretty much a counseling session in which I quickly became weighed down. I used to finish my hour of calls feeling like I wanted to go wallow in mud and sorrows (which, ironically, weren't even my own sorrows, but the sorrows of others that I had picked up during prayer) and eat a big block of chocolate while finding a quiet room and shutting the door to the world for the rest of the day. I didn't understand how to cast off that weight in prayer then. So this terminology of *burdens in prayer* has always perplexed me. Why would God tell us that we are to bear one another's burdens when it seems very counterproductive to His easy yoke and light burden?

Well, that's because the English language has translated those two verses with the same word, *burden*, when in actual fact they are two completely separate Greek words that, while similar, have separate meanings. The word for the "easy burden" in Matthew 11:30 is the Greek word, *phortion*, which is defined as "an invoice as part of the freight of a ship, a task or a service, or burden" (Strong's, G5413). It paints the picture of you and me being like a merchant ship that is carrying an invoice of merchandise on board, but it is light for the ship to carry. I see it as the task of every believer to be like that merchant ship where we deliver "the good news" and heaven's solutions through our specific calling and destiny, but it is not a heavy task. It is easy for the ship to carry. I want you to understand the context of this verse in order to understand the context of the next. Jesus is asking you:

> *Are you weary, carrying a heavy burden? Then come to me. I will refresh your life, for I am your oasis. Simply join your life with mine. Learn my ways and you'll discover that I'm gentle, humble, easy to please. You will find refreshment and rest in me. For all that I require of you will be pleasant and easy to bear* (Matthew 11:28-30).

The Greek translation of the words from verse 29 says, "take up the beam of My balance, bear My *rest*." In *The Passion Translation* footnotes, it says that this verse can also be read, "bend your neck to my yoke." It is the picture of an ox coming alongside another ox and bending their necks together to carry the plow. This is actually a picture of prophetic prayer, bending ourselves to Jesus, and together we carry the burden of prayer. The difference is Jesus is the stronger ox that carries the load, the weight of the world, while you get to "bear His rest" as you walk alongside Him in this journey of prophetic prayer.

On the other hand, when in actual reference to prayer or intercession, "burden" in the verse of Galatians 6:2 has a different Greek word. Let's read the scripture and the verse before it as a whole so we can understand its context:

> Brothers, if anyone is caught in any sin, you who are spiritual [that is, you who are responsive to the guidance of the Spirit] are to restore such a person in a spirit of gentleness [not with a sense of superiority or self-righteousness], keeping a watchful eye on yourself, so that you are not tempted as well. Carry one another's burdens and in this way you will fulfill the requirements of the law of Christ [that is, the law of Christian love] (Galatians 6:1-2 AMP).

This is the verse that has been taken out of context where many believe that it is a sign of spiritual authority to walk around forlorn and cast down in prayer as we "carry each other's burdens." But the English word *burden* and the Greek word used here do not correlate the same meaning. Let us first take a look at the English definition for the word *burden*: "something difficult or unpleasant that you have to deal with or worry about: the burden of responsibility."[2] The Greek word that is used in this verse, however, is *baros* and it means "abundance of authority that makes a demand on one's resources, whether physical or spiritual" (Strong's, G922). While it does denote "burden," it does not define it in the way the English language does. Strong's Concordance describes it as an eternal weight of glory.

Baros also comes from the Greek root word of *basis*, which means "base or a step." Can you see the stark contrast here? To give you a better understanding of this verse and, ultimately, our assignment in prophetic prayer, let us look at the Greek word used for "carry" in this verse. It is the word *bastazo*, which is defined as "the idea of removal, to lift, to declare, to carry and take up" (Strong's, G941). Notice that this call to take up authority is speaking to those of us who are in the Spirit, who recognize a brother who is lost or caught in sin. Let's read those two verses with the Greek translations inserted:

> *Brothers, if anyone is caught in any sin, you who are spiritual [that is, you who are responsive to the guidance of the Spirit] are to restore such a person in a spirit of gentleness [not with a sense of superiority or self-righteousness], keeping a watchful eye on yourself, so that you are not tempted as well.* [Lift up, declare and remove] *one another's **burdens*** [through the abundance of your authority, make a demand on your spiritual resources], *and in this way you will fulfil the requirements of the law of Christ [that is, the law of Christian love].*

Where the Greek word *baros* can also mean basis or step, consider that when you release your authority and declare in prayer on their behalf you are in actuality taking a step of faith for them where they have become caught and lost their own way. Prophetic prayer isn't weighed down by burdens but by glory. I see it this way—a king or queen who is walking into the royal courts is laden with a gold crown, a royal robe, and scepter. The king or queen is not weighed down by these items they wear, but rather they are the symbols of their authority and they walk with their heads held high. Likewise, the assignment of prophetic prayer is the scepter of your authority in Christ. Don't allow the enemy to convince you for one second longer that prayer is a difficult or unpleasant burden to carry. Remind him that your assignment in prayer is to release the weight of God's glory that rests upon you, to decree and declare the end from the beginning, to remove the burdens of others through the abundance of your authority in Christ, and to fulfill the law of Christ—which is the law of Christian love. Prophetic prayer is indeed the act of Christian love. To prophetically rewrite a story of brokenness into wholeness. To establish the reign of His kingdom and spread the mandate of Isaiah 61, which says:

> *The mighty Spirit of Lord Yahweh is wrapped around me*
> *because Yahweh has anointed me,*
> *as a messenger to preach good news to the poor.*
> *He sent me to heal the wounds of the brokenhearted,*
> *to tell captives, "You are free,"*
> *and to tell prisoners, "Be free from your darkness"*
> (Isaiah 61:1).

PROPHETIC SOLUTION KEY #9

Pray with God's glory.

Prayer shouldn't be a burden, but a release of God's glory that is resting on you. Be alert to the enemy using an assignment in prayer against you by trying to make you feel weighed down by it. Cast off any weight and receive the grace of Jesus to walk in your assigned calling to decree the answers of God.

NOTES

1. Clay Wilson, "Improvised Explosive Devices (IEDs) in Iraq: Effects and Countermeasures," Naval History and Heritage Command, August 10, 2018, https://www.history.navy.mil/research/library/online -reading-room/title-list-alphabetically/i/improvised-explosive-devices-in -iraq-effects-and-countermeasures.html.

2. "Burden," in *Cambridge Dictionary*, https://dictionary.cambridge.org/ us/dictionary/english/burden.

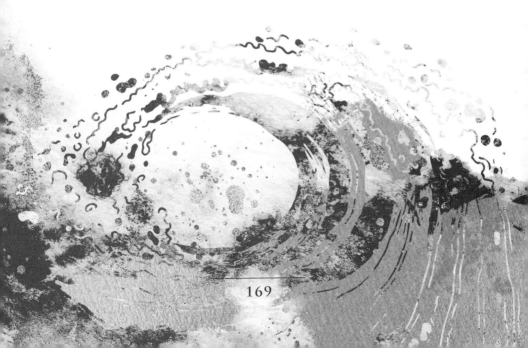

PART FOUR

RELEASING GOD'S HEART

CHAPTER TEN

RELEASING
HIS VOICE

One of my favorite stories to learn from in the Bible is the story of the Exodus. I personally find there is so much to learn within this story of the Israelites' mass migration. It is a story I never tire of because every time I read it, I see another lesson, another perspective of how we can learn to seize and activate God's promises and answers within our own lives and move into our own promised lands. One of the biggest mistakes I believe the Israelites made that ultimately stalled the conquest of their promised land was their whining and complaining. You can't really blame them, though—they had lived a life of slavery, and therefore the way they perceived everything was through the eyes of a slave, not a son or daughter. No sooner had the waters of the Red Sea receded and their enemies washed away did they again complain. "What now? Has God led us out of slavery into desolation?" Slaves live with a victim and survival mindset. They couldn't see the Red Sea for what it was because all they could see was what lay ahead—a desert wasteland.

If they had celebrated the victory behind them, perhaps they would have seen what was truly ahead of them—that God would make a way for them through the desert. Instead, they whined.

Have you ever been in the presence of a child when they are whining?

I remember when my daughters were both very little, in their toddler years, and there was a phase both of them went through (and sometimes they still need reminding that they have surpassed this stage). The whining phase—I remember it being the most testing, trying time of my life as a parent thus far. When Nate was working a 9 to 5 job, I would be at home alone and, therefore, their only source of having needs met. It was the phase where they didn't yet understand how to communicate their feelings, and I remember many days when they would be whining and crying at my feet, for usually the most trivial of reasons. Everything within me wanted to run away and hide during that phase. They would get frustrated if they weren't understood and their voice would turn into this monotone, endless whine. Because I had two little ones with not a large age gap between them, I was exasperated until one day I was watching our friend Seth Dahl on Facebook talk about how he deals with whining. He said he would get down on their level and show them through a calm response, "This is what I want your voice to sound like. Can you hear how I sound? When your voice sounds like mine, then I can listen to you."

I believe this is a key for activating God's answers. When we are looking at a problem through the lens of survival, we sound like a whining child. "What are You going to do, God? How are You going to fix this? What next?" However, when we change our perspective, our voice and authority dramatically change too. We learn how to release the answers as He does. When we see the problem through the lens of a miracle-working God, we are able to speak differently, and our voice ends up sounding like His. Evidently, we can see through the story of Exodus that God is not a fan of whining either, but it goes much deeper than whining in itself. The Israelites' mentality was one of slavery, which came out through the sound of their complaints. God knew that with that mindset they could not handle the size of the promises that awaited them. In fact, the enormity of the blessing would probably kill them, so He patiently waited for them to change their tune. Forty years later, they stubbornly refused to change their whines into thankfulness.

How you perceive God and how you look at problems can tell you a lot about whether or not you have been thinking with the mentality of a son or daughter or through a slavery mindset. The two are incompatible. If we are to walk with authority upon the earth, we are going to have to sustain what we release. We can't just release answers and then not be able to sustain them. I believe God is growing us up in this area so that we can hold with ease the fulfillment of promises that have been promised to this very generation. When you are able to look at a desolate wasteland that stands in front of you and rather than complain about it you see it as an opportunity to call down miraculous rain, you know that you are ready to move.

One of the biggest keys to activating the prophetic solutions and answers of heaven is to see as He sees, speak as He speaks, and move as He moves. I encourage you to pause for a moment and ask the Holy Spirit these questions: "Have I been seeing problems through the mindset of survival? If so, I lay down that way of thinking and I pick up my faith once again. Teach me and help me to move as You move and to speak as You speak." I believe this generation that is alive right now is a Joshua generation. A people who don't whine at the size of a problem but seize it with the authority of Christ and command the giants to bow.

AUTHORING WITH CHRIST

Unfortunately, Moses and an entire generation of the Israelites were never able to learn this valuable lesson and, therefore, were unable to cross into their awaited promise. Joshua, on the other hand, was one of the two spies who saw the land and said, "Let's go, we are well able to seize it." The Father is looking for a people who will wholeheartedly partner with what He is speaking and then release His life-giving words into the earth that will set off a cataclysmic chain of events to rewrite every wrong. We must move as Joshua did and respond with faith to what God is speaking.

In the first chapter of the Book of Joshua, Moses had just died, and the reigns of authority now rested in the hands of Joshua. The Lord then spoke to Joshua and told him, *"I will give you every place where you set your foot, as I promised Moses"* (Josh. 1:3 NIV). I want you to think on this statement for a moment. Every place your foot treads. The question must be asked then, does this scripture apply to you and me in the here and now as well? Or is it merely a Bible verse meant for Joshua in that time alone? I want to share an excerpt from Dutch Sheets' book *Authority in Prayer* that details the answer to this question with keen insight. He writes:

Before we endeavor to move forward in understanding our personal authority in Christ, however, we must first look at His ultimate authority over the earth as Creator. This is the foundation all of our governmental prayers must be built upon. I was somewhat surprised when I looked up the word *authority* in my older Webster's dictionary, a huge ancient one passed down from my dad—so big that I think it doubled as a weapon. At first I couldn't find *authority* in it. Puzzled, I kept looking. Then I saw it, tucked away under the various derivatives and definitions of the word *author*. The root concept behind authority is authorship, not as in writing but as in origination or creation. One has authority over what one authors. A creator determines the purpose of his creation and holds all rights to it. God, of course, is creative—it is His nature. And how can a creator not create? So the great Creator went to work, and the first two chapters of Genesis describe the results. One verse in particular describes His pleasure over the outcome: "God saw all that He had made, and behold, it was very good" (1:31). That God is author and Creator of the earth and all it contains settles the issue of ultimate authority over it. Jesus has always maintained His ownership and authority. (Again, the authority He won back at Calvary was what Adam lost, not His own.) ...Establishing this fact that Christ is Creator and Owner—and therefore, the ultimate authority—of all is critical if we are to truly pray with authority and legislate through intercession.[1]

I found this revelation of authority amazing. Our authority in Christ, more simply put, is legislating over what is already His. What was lost through the fall of Adam was restored through Christ, and now can be fully redeemed through you and me. We are the legislators of heaven, stewarding our initial mandate to subdue the earth. We are the gatekeepers and watchmen over the earth who have been given the incredible opportunity to author the original designs of God. So, the answer to that question above is yes, the mandate for Joshua is the same for you and me: "*I will give you every place where you set your foot, as I promised Moses.*" If the earth is the Lord's and everything that is in it (see Ps. 24:1) and all of Jesus' authority is rightfully back in His hands (see Matt. 28:18) and He has released us into the earth as His disciples, carrying the full weight of that authority—what then could the earth look like if we fully moved in this powerful and life-changing revelation? I get the feeling that we haven't seen anything yet. We are privileged to live in amazing days to create with Him.

Can you begin to see areas of your own life in your family, your city, and your nation where you can see how God can author a solution out of a problem? Is your heart starting to creatively come alive as you imagine heaven released into those situations and regions? On earth as it is in heaven. That statement is not God's wishful thinking for the earth—it is His heart intention. All it takes is for you and me to run with it—wholeheartedly. If we begin to look like, sound like, and author like Him, what could our cities and regions begin to look like as well? Poverty would begin to turn into wealth and abundance—because there is no poverty in heaven. Sickness would dissipate, hospitals would be emptied—because there is no sickness in heaven. Drugs would be eradicated—because people would no longer be looking to fill their voids with substance, but they would turn and run into Him. Prostitution, human trafficking, abortion, and every other grave injustice would be in history books. Is it possible? Yes. Does it sound far reaching and crazy to even imagine? Absolutely. But our God is a God of the impossible and I do believe that all it takes is one person who says, "God, I want to look like, sound like, and move like You. May my life be Your vessel which You speak through."

DISARMING THE REIGN OF TERROR

What took place in Mumbai, India all those years ago (the story of Chhatrapati Shivaji Terminus from Chapter Six), has forever stayed with me. I no longer want to be someone who prays to protect myself alone; I want to be someone who strikes heaven into the earth and leaves a mark. I want my life to count for something in heaven. In the years following that experience, I began to drive around neighborhoods and prophesy that His glory would be poured out. I began to look for ways to release His kingdom and search them out. It wouldn't be until a number of years later that a similar opportunity would arise, and this time I knew what to do with it.

Nate and I were with our two girls, Charlotte and Sophie, ministering together in New York City. As you have read in Chapter Six about discerning the atmospheres over regions with your spirit, you may know what I mean when I say that New York can feel very heavy. This is not a declaration over New York. However, it tells me what God longs to do in and through this city. He wants to rewrite it for

His glory. We had just come from Washington D.C. where we had been praying over the Supreme Court, and the issue of abortion was heavy on my mind. I knew the extremely high statistics of abortion in the city and suddenly I was confronted with the heavy realization of the spirit that was lingering all around. I began to notice the lack of children on the streets of New York, and my heart was grieved. It felt like we were walking right in the middle of a bizarre movie, and to make it even stranger some people were looking at our daughters as though they had never seen a child in their lives.

I've been to the city multiple times but never noticed this before. This time felt different. Maybe it was because I was in a hyper-sensitive state of alert having just come from the Supreme Court, so I spent much of the time walking the streets just praying in tongues. Praying in tongues is an incredible weapon in our artillery, especially when you don't know what to pray or to help you refrain from speaking negativity when that is all you can feel. I remember asking the Father to show me His heart for the city, because in that moment all I felt was grief and anger combined. I heard His whisper, "Mercy. Redemption." So I prayed into that, saying, "Jesus, I release Your mercy over this city. I release Your mercy over the innocent bloodshed. I speak God's redemption to you, New York City."

I highlight this to you because, as I mentioned earlier in this chapter, when we perceive God's heart through the wrong lens it distorts our ability to author His heart. I'm thankful that in that moment I leaned into His heart and heard His whisperings of mercy and redemption; otherwise, I might have interpreted what I was about to perceive in a very different light. It was October of 2017 that we were visiting, and we were staying close to the heart of Times

Square. We wanted to take a trip down to Greenwich Village to try some food places that I had found on Instagram—namely, a pizza place and a donut store (let's just say we were on a foodie tour, or "oh taste and see" trip).

As we were walking to our closest subway station on 41st Street right next to Times Square, I remember feeling a sense of alarm as a long procession of police cars with their sirens on screamed passed us, right as we were about to enter the subway. We entered in and I took a photo of the 41st Street station because that's what you do when you're a tourist—you take a photo of everything that looks even slightly interesting, even if it's a dirty subway. We went down the escalators, swiped our subway cards through the turnstiles, and began walking toward our train number. I have to add I was still feeling that sense of alert and I wasn't sure why. As we made our way through the large underground system, I suddenly walked into that same wall of terror that I had felt in Mumbai some nine years earlier.

Nate was rushing a little ahead of me with Sophie in his arms and Charlotte was hand in hand with me. We were running slightly late for our train and we wanted to make sure we caught it, or we would have to wait around 30 minutes for the next one to take us to our destination. Thirty minutes is a long time to be waiting underground with a four- and six-year-old. Yet none of this mattered as soon as I felt that wall of terror. I called out to Nate, "I have to pray. I can sense that same terror I felt in Mumbai. I don't know why, but we have to stop right here so I can pray." If I had not heard the heart of God for New York about His mercy and redemption, I could have perceived this feeling of terror in one of two ways:

RELEASING PROPHETIC SOLUTIONS

1. I could have assumed that this was the effect of sin, that terror was running rampant in its streets and what could I possibly do to alter that?

2. I could have just walked away from that feeling of terror and assumed that sin deserved judgement.

Thankfully, I had leaned into His heart and knew that it was within my authority to legislate heaven, right where I stood, as odd as it seemed. So, I dropped my bag in between my feet and, feeling like a crazed person, began to prophesy out loud. I remember decreeing these words: "Terror, I speak to you, you have no place or right here. I speak the Blood of Jesus over New York City. I disarm the plans of the enemy and I speak the mercy and redemption of God. I claim Psalm 91 over its streets, above and below." I then remember releasing angels on assignment to protect the city as a whole, not just over me and my family, but I released His kingdom into the entire city. I can tell you, it did not feel holy or spiritual by any means. I felt stupid. It wasn't that I was yelling, but I knew there was a certain authority that was demanded to be released. I spoke the solution of God into the atmosphere until I felt that burden, or rather weight of His glory released from me and into the subway where I stood.

THE BLOOD OF JESUS
SPEAKS A BETTER WORD

It grieves my heart when I see a word released in the name of prophecy with the connotations of God's judgment over a person, city, or country. For example, when a natural disaster takes place, social media often becomes flooded with "words" of judgement. Only very recently, my own country of Australia faced an extreme season of bushfires. In the wake of worldwide attention, I noticed numerous words circulating social media with titles like, "God's judgment upon Australia." In a time when our country was needing prayer, empathy, and support, words of condemnation did not help anyone or anything, and in my opinion they only further pushed people away from God. I want to briefly highlight the view of God's judgment in the New Testament, because without understanding it we run the risk of releasing our words as weapons of death and destruction rather than life and mercy. In light of Australia's bushfires, I do want to highlight something: both New South Wales and Victoria—the two states hardest hit by fires—had issued extremely sinful laws mere months before the bushfires erupted with fury.

One law was unrestricted abortion to birth and the other was euthanasia—both were laws of death. Romans tells us that *"the wages of sin is death, but the gift of God is eternal life in Jesus Christ"* (Rom. 6:23 NKJV). Sin does indeed bear consequences and the only fruit that it can produce is death. Do I believe that the fires were in some way connected to these laws? Yes. While there were many factors that led to the fires, my answer remains. You cannot sow death and reap life. Do I believe the bushfires were a result of God's judgment? No. The wages of sin is a judgment unto itself. That is what the law came to reveal—that sin without redemption was its own judgment. Yes, God is a judge, and He is a righteous judge, but if it was His true desire to punish people, as many of these words reveal, why did He send Jesus to die in our place, even while we were yet dead in our sins? He would be contradicting Himself. I am not suggesting every natural calamity is the result of sin; however, in this instance, it was too obvious to ignore.

John 10:10 clearly tells us that God is the life-giver and satan is the life-stealer. But where sin prevails without repentance, God simply cannot move. That is, until you and I step into the narrative. This doesn't mean we turn a blind eye to sin, but should we simply agree with sin and its wages and make declarations by our own self-righteousness? "That's what they deserve! This is the result of God's judgment." Or should we extend the same kiss of mercy to them that we have received? As I was praying over our nation of Australia and considering all of this, the Holy Spirit reminded me of this verse:

> If My people who are called by My name will humble themselves, and pray and seek My face, and turn from their wicked ways, then I will hear from heaven, and will forgive their sin and heal their land (2 Chronicles 7:14 NKJV).

In this verse, God gives us a significant key to prophetic prayer that we need to pay attention to. He doesn't instruct the lost sinners to pray and turn from their wicked ways, but rather His own people. It indicates that the sons and daughters are to wear the responsibility of the sins of the nations as their own, whether they have walked in wickedness or not. Rather than pointing the blame outward, we say, "Father, forgive *us*." When we do this, it releases a sound that is heard in heaven where God issues forgiveness and ushers in the Blood of Jesus to heal the land (or the people in question). It's you and me who are the tide-changers. How do we know that this is

God's plan under the New Covenant? Because, as Paul writes, *"And we have come to Jesus who established a **new covenant** with his blood sprinkled upon the mercy seat; blood that continues to speak from heaven, 'forgiveness,' a better message than Abel's blood that cries from the earth, 'justice'"* (Heb. 12:24).

We see here that Abel's blood cries for justice and vengeance, but when God's people humble themselves and pray, bearing the responsibility of the sin, and ask God to forgive them, the Blood of Jesus that speaks "forgiveness" voids the contract with the "wages of sin" under the Old Testament law. When our own church prayed in this manner over Australia, we saw healing rain fall upon the land within days. Rain fell over ferocious and relentless fires, washing them away; rain filled dams that had been dry for years. The Blood of Jesus spoke a better word of forgiveness and mercy rained down. It's that simple.

Proverbs tells us that *"A nation is exalted by the righteousness of its people, but sin heaps disgrace upon the land"* (Prov. 14:34). So, which is it? Does righteousness reign or does sin? When I exercise my gift of righteousness as His daughter and co-author mercy's kiss with Him, righteousness covers the sin that once stained the land. Does this mean I am suggesting we allow people to continue in sin? Do we ignore these sins, like the abortion and euthanasia laws in my country? Absolutely not. We move in active opposition to sin on one hand, and with the other hand we extend the kiss of mercy to the people and the land. This is where I believe many do not fully understand the judgment of God under the New Covenant. We can know His heart by looking at what Jesus said to the Pharisees:

*"Healthy people don't need to see a doctor, but the sick will
go for treatment." Then he added, "Now you should go and
study the meaning of the verse: I want you to show mercy,
not just offer me a sacrifice"* (Matthew 9:12-13).

We cannot forget that this is the same kindness that saved and
redeemed us, and it is this same standard that we are required to
represent. It is His kindness that leads the lost to Jesus (see Rom.
2:4). It's His desire to show mercy through us, not so that people go
on sinning unrestrained but so that they can have another chance
to be found and redeemed by Him. Not only are we gatekeepers of
heaven on earth, we stand as gatekeepers blocking the gates of hell
to the lost. I remembered the cost of not praying this way last time.

As I stood in the subway of New York, I continued to pray in
tongues until I discerned that the feeling of terror had lifted. As
soon as it did, I picked up my bag, grabbed Charlotte's hand, and
off we ran to our train, which, I am happy to tell you, we still made
in time. That in itself was a miracle, which to this day I believe
God held back time for us in that split moment. But it would
not be until six weeks later when we were back in Australia that
I would realize the weight of the prayer that day. I received a call
from my mum, "Have you seen the news this morning? Weren't
you just staying near Times Square in New York?" I quickly turned
on the news, which I rarely ever watch, and immediately saw news
reports of an attempted terrorism attack were splashing all over
the screen. My mouth dropped when the location was revealed.
The 41st Street subway station. They showed pictures of multitudes
of police cars with their sirens out front, just as I had seen that
particular morning when we were there. They then began to share

details how a suicide bomber had created a pipe bomb that he had planned to detonate underground and attempt to kill hundreds of people alongside him.

Scenes began to emerge of moments before the attempted detonation, and although I couldn't make it out clearly, it looked almost identical to the spot where I had prayed just weeks earlier. Though I can't be certain of that exact location, I am sure of this—the bomb failed to detonate as planned, something went wrong. There were a handful of people who suffered minor injuries, but what should have been a fatal event was not. The pipe bomb failed to detonate as he had planned. I knew that God had sent us into that station that day to pray and release His solution into the atmosphere. Prayer knows no bounds and it is not restricted by time. I wholeheartedly know and believe that angels were released that day with the assignment to detonate the plans of incoming terror. They waited there until that very moment to intervene and halt the plans of the enemy. Why? Who knows that if many of those people who might have been killed in that attempt might have not yet known Him?

I believe God's solutions are much bigger than our own. They extend beyond our reaches and limits of time, space, and atmosphere; and they invade into the moments they are needed. I want to remind you that you have the same authority in Christ, the same capacity to discern the heart of God and release His mercy and solutions. I am not some special case but, rather, a testimony of what you too are gifted to walk in. I want to encourage you—begin to ask the Holy Spirit to reveal to you areas in your own life, your family, your city, and your nation where He wants you to partner with Him and author His mercy with Him. I believe it is within our grasp to ask the Holy Spirit to show us something to release for each and every day. As it is written:

> *If you wait at wisdom's doorway,*
>
> *longing to hear a word for every day,*
>
> *joy will break forth within you as you listen for what I'll say.*
>
> *For the fountain of life pours into you every time that you find me,*
>
> *and this is the secret of growing in the delight*
>
> *and the favor of the Lord*
>
> (Proverbs 8:34-35).

The first sentence of this verse can also be translated to say, "Guard the door of My entrances," which takes us back to our role as gatekeepers and watchmen. When we ask Him and long to hear a word for every day, it releases His joy. What a beautiful picture of partnership and authoring with Him. I can find no greater privilege than to release Him. How about you?

PROPHETIC SOLUTION KEY #10

Pray with mercy's kiss.

You are called to author with Christ, just as Adam authored the names of the animals in the Garden of Eden. Your role in the New Covenant is to author solutions with Him by His mercy. Where do you see in your life, your family, culture, and in the nations that needs to be authored anew by His name? Begin to use your authority to decree as He decrees and release His heart into every sphere.

NOTE

1. Sheets, *Authority in Prayer.*

CHAPTER ELEVEN

STRIKE THE GROUND

"Vision is the power that sustains. Whatever we keep in front of our eyes is what will determine our outcome!"[1]

Have you ever prayed over a situation that looks outwardly impossible, and no matter how much you pray it continues to visibly remain seemingly immovable? God calls us to have a type of faith that defiantly resists impossibilities. A type of bold, offensive faith that stares down the laws of what physically may appear immovable and command it to bow to His name. It's this kind of faith that pleases Him. Hebrews 11:6 tells us, *"And without faith living within us it would be impossible to please God. For we come to God in faith knowing that he is real and that he rewards the faith of those who give all their passion and strength into seeking him."*

Abraham needed faith to seize the impossible promise of his child in his old age. Noah needed faith to build the ark despite the ongoing echoes of mockery from those all around him. David needed faith to take down the giant when all the rest of Israel were too afraid to confront him. Daniel needed faith to continue worshiping God despite the threat of being thrown in the lions' den. Shadrach,

Meshach, and Abednego needed faith to trust God as they refused to bow down to the idol—their faith carried them into, through, and out of the fire. Unfortunately, all too many give up in this process of what I like to call "striking the ground." It is the process of persistent, defiant prayer when all seems hopeless, impossible, and immovable.

When God calls us to a mission of prayer over a situation, we often start out excited, with all guns blazing and ready to cast this mountain into the sea. However, after multiple strikes and no obvious change, we far too quickly give up. What many don't realize is releasing prophetic prayer is a deployment. A period of time when you have been moved into a position to contend and call down the kingdom of God into the situation and region where you have been placed. As you have read in this book, I have had many moments of instant breakthroughs, but there are other assignments that I have been deployed to pray into that I am still contending for to this day. A calling to prophetic prayer is not an overnight, microwave, magic potion; it is the lifestyle of a servant-soldier, a laid-down lover of the King who has said in his or her heart, "I will lay my life down for this." It is the daily choice to surrender your will to His, and in doing so He uses your life as an arrow to strike and strike again at the stubborn rocks of resistance. Your life becomes the very tool that breaks the enemy into pieces, but you have to be willing to be in it for both the short and the long haul, knowing that His grace will sustain you.

At the time of writing this, we have just returned to Australia from a four-week-long ministry trip in the United States with our two girls in tow. Travel, ministry, and parenting combined, while simultaneously orchestrating online courses, is no easy task, so allow me to just say from the outset that I am not typically one who has this magical ability to escape the snares of jet lag. Maybe it's because of how much we do, but instead of bouncing back like an energizer bunny, jet lag often lulls me into its sleepy trance. It usually takes me a number of days to emerge out of its clutches where I am able to feel like a normal human being again. I also tend to dream nightly, but when jet lag hits, I neither dream nor remember where I am or who I am and find that my sleep is more like a coma than an ordinary night's rest.

Our first night arriving back was oddly different though. Where I usually hit the pillow like a sack of concrete, this night my mind was a buzzing hive of thoughts. Nate and I are currently on the verge of crossing into a long-awaited promise of moving to the United States, a promise that God gave us ten years ago, and we are in the final process of coming back to Australia to tie up all the details with the plan to return permanently to the United States within a few months. As I fell asleep early one afternoon, I felt a sense of fear sweep over me with the thoughts racing through my mind, "What if it all doesn't work out? What if the home you found and fell in love with doesn't work out? What if your visas don't go through like you think they will?" Right at that moment, I knew I had a decision to make, even in the midst of my jet lagged state of mind. All of these "what ifs" were trying to entice my authority into submissive defeat.

"Holy Spirit, what do You say about this?" I asked Him wearily. I then heard His simple but clear reply, *"Send in the battering ram."* I shot up straight in bed in surprise. What an odd thought—a battering ram. I vaguely understood what He was saying and simply replied, "Okay, Lord, whatever You say," and in my tiredness I fell back onto my pillow and went straight to sleep. All night long I dreamed of those words as the Holy Spirit whispered them directly into my ear, "Send in the battering ram." This in itself was unusual as I rarely dream when I am this tired. So when I woke up at 3 AM the following morning (thank you, jet lag), it was all I could think about. "The battering ram."

A quick Google search revealed its definition in Merriam-Webster's dictionary: "a military siege engine consisting of a large wooden beam with a head of iron used in ancient times to beat down the walls of a besieged place."[2] I wrote this in a prophetic word after receiving further revelation about the battering ram:

> You're likely familiar with the picture of a battering ram if you've ever watched a war movie of any kind. It's a large beam-like structure with a pointed head, generally made of iron, hinged upon a pendulum device and it is used by an invading army to break down a wall or door. The invading army will align their battering ram with the entrance of the fortified structure that they want to break into and they will begin pulling back the beam which will swing forward with force into the target. They will repeat this until finally, the fortified door breaks down. I find it amazing that the head of the battering ram is generally made out of iron. In Psalm 2:9 it speaks of Jesus wielding a rod of iron saying, "And you will shepherd them with unlimited authority, crushing their rebellion as an iron rod smashes jars of clay!" Did you catch that? Iron biblically represents your authority in Christ. Jesus *is* the battering ram who breaks through the enemy's rebellion. In Genesis 22:13,

Abraham discovered a ram caught in the thicket and used the ram as a sacrifice in place of his son. The ram prophetically points to Jesus, the battering ram stuck in the thicket on our behalf. He has gone before you and made a way for you into your promised land. You can know with confidence today that you are *not* stuck, for He was stuck for you. His blood has become that iron head of a weapon that will break down any obstacle and breach that stands between you and your promise.[3]

Did you catch that? Iron biblically represents your authority. The Hebrew word for "rod" in this scripture is the word *shebet*, which points to a scepter or a mark of authority (Strong's, H7626). What is the rebellion this scripture is speaking of though? It is the rebellion of the enemy. Anything that you see that does not line up with the Word of God and the finished work of the cross is the work of the rebellion of the enemy.

It always grieves my heart when I hear people say that they have received an illness from God so that He can teach them something in it. Jesus never gave sickness; He always healed people of their illnesses. If you don't see it in Jesus and if you don't see it in the finished work of the cross, then you can know for sure that it is the workings of rebellion from the enemy. This can apply to every area of our lives, both personally and to nations. If there is terror ruling and reigning over a nation, you can know for certain that you have been given the authority of Christ to cast it out (see 1 John 4:17). You have His authority to smash any rebellion and command it to align with His will. The key is found in consistency.

The battering ram was modeled after a male sheep, a ram that is fighting his opponent for territory. The ram will hit his opponent repetitively until his contender either backs down or dies. You and I need to have that same resilience and steadfastness as the battering ram—to look at the door of impossibility and smash it over and over with the Word of God. I believe we are the generation that was prophesied about in Psalm 24:6: "*Such is the generation of those who seek him, who seek your face, God of Jacob*" (NIV). We are the generation that will see a mighty outpouring sweep across the earth, not because we are lying on our backs passively but because we are the likeness of Jesus, the battering ram of heaven, who does not back down. We are the generation that refuses to give up and we are taking back territory that has long been in the enemy's clutches. An outpouring of His glory will come by way of our contending, not by our works but by our fervor and passion to see our King glorified. We need to look at the impossibilities that we face all around us and hold up our siege engine of promise and decree what He has spoken, striking it again and again until we see the Word smash the impossibilities like a jar of clay.

THE POWER OF "CONTINUE"

In Revelation 2, Jesus sends a letter to each of the churches. His letter to the church named Thyatira is particularly interesting. *Thyatira* means "continual sacrifice." The context of Jesus' letter to this particular church gives us greater understanding of this meaning and how it adds depth to the battering ram. Jesus talks to the church of Thyatira about avoiding the practices of Jezebel. If you have been around church circles long enough, you will know that Jezebel is a commonly used name. Interestingly, however, many within the church in our day and age may know of her name but are misconceived about the reality of what and who she is. There are common misconceptions that women teachers or women prophets are operating in the spirit of Jezebel or that every woman who walks in any kind of authority has this trait. Let's clear something up. Jezebel is not in the form of a human being in our present time; she is a demonic principality—though humans may indeed be possessed by her, scripture does not tell us that all women are therefore of Jezebel. It is a spirit of this age and it is not difficult to see. Jezebel is a principality of seduction. She seduces by means of sexuality, unauthorized authority, distraction, confusion, mockery, and sacrifice. We see this principality is prevalent in today's society where generations are obsessed with body image, sexuality, sexual identity, feminism, distraction, confusion, mockery of Jesus, and even through the common child sacrificial practices of abortion. How much of this has been tolerated by the Church as a whole? How long have we stood off to the side, afraid to confront what is right in front of our eyes? We have chosen tolerance as acceptance, and we must decide to change that decision. We must decide to take back the reins of society through our God-given authority and remove the ranks of this principality's unauthorized authority. We must take back what rightfully belongs to us as inherent sons and daughters of the King. Yes, we are to do it in love, but love should never be translated as tolerance.

I wonder, how long have we been lulled into a state of "modernism" that we have tolerated the ways of Jezebel in our lives and nations without even realizing it? Much like jet lag, we have grown weary and exhausted in our efforts of well-doing, and just like those simple but sneaky "what ifs" that tried to gain my agreement, many have made a transaction of agreement with an inferior truth. Through our agreement with a simple but destructive lie, we have handed the rights of a generation to Jezebel's control. In our tired, exhausted, and distracted states, far too many have allowed the poisonous wisdom of the world to pollute their beliefs of truth like a cancer. We have believed the lie that acceptance and tolerance is love, and in doing so it has disarmed our authority. What we have failed to recognize is, our God-given authority isn't just for us and our own benefit; it is for the people of the earth.

I believe that Jesus' words to the church of Thyatira are indeed speaking to the modern-day Church that has largely tolerated Jezebel. We have lost sight of what rightfully belongs to us and to the kingdom of God, and by tolerance we have handed over the scepter of iron to an inferior and illegal seductress. This is important to understand, because if we allow these beliefs to continue to seduce us we will forget what we are actually fighting for and we will turn into a tolerating lamb rather than a battering ram. This doesn't mean we batter down people. We batter down the enemy who is holding this world in his unworthy grip. It's time to take back what was rightfully given into our hands—the discipling of nations. We have tolerated the beliefs of the world for far too long, which has essentially disarmed our authority in Christ and moved us into passivity rather than activity.

Read carefully the words of Jesus to Thyatira:

> *Cling tightly to all that you have until I appear. To everyone who is victorious and continues to do my works to the very end I will give you authority over the nations to*

shepherd them with a royal scepter. And the rebellious will be shattered as clay pots—even as I also received authority from the presence of my Father. I will give the morning star to the one who experiences victory (Revelation 2:25-28).

Our God-given authority was not given into our hands so that we would march around in prideful arrogance like a dictator, but it was given that we might serve the earth as dispensers of His glory, that all may see and know Him through us. Notice Jesus said *cling tightly*. Just like the battering ram, we are to hold tightly to the promises He has given us, both personally and on a larger scale. Then it says, *"to everyone who is victorious and **continues** to do my works to the very end I will give you authority over the nations."* That word *continues* is where many lose sight. We fail to continue in truth. We fail to continue to keep the promise before our eyes. We fail to continue in persistence to see what He has promised in the supernatural eventuate in the natural. However, we find victory over this principality, and every other demonic principality in hell, *when* we *continue*. It is amazing that *Thyatira* means "continual sacrifice." It tells me that our ability to continue in prayer becomes like a sacrifice on the altar of worship to our King. It pleases Him when we continue.

THE POWER OF "RESIST"

James 4:7 puts it simply like this: *"So then, surrender to God. Stand up to the devil and resist him and he will turn and run away from you."*

The Greek word used for *resist* here is the word *anthistémi*. It is a compound word where *anti* means "to oppose against" and *hístēmi* means "to take a complete stand against, a 180-degree, contrary position" (Strong's, G436). To establish one's position publicly by conspicuously "holding one's ground," refusing to be moved ("pushed back"). It also means to oppose fully, to forcefully declare one's personal conviction where they unswervingly stand, to keep one's possession, ardently withstand without giving up (letting go).

It was also a *military* term in classical Greek meaning "to strongly resist an opponent." I find it intriguing that one of the definitions for this word means to "establish publicly by conspicuously holding one's ground," which is ironic if we bring into consideration the principality of Jezebel, which causes the Church to run and hide from confrontation rather than directly opposing her. I'm not just referring to Jezebel either, but in this day and age what we do in secret will be displayed in public. We can no longer passively oppose issues like abortion, but we must be confronting these issues publicly and boldly. I am not suggesting to do this without wisdom, but when we apply all of the principles I have been showing you, we resist satan with the solutions of heaven, and we do so with a strong stance to not give up until we see his walls of fortification fall. We should be holding a contrary position to the world, not one that agrees with it. We can love the people of the without agreeing with them. It is when we have this stance of direct opposition to satan, refusing to let up or let go, that we will cause him and his minions like Jezebel to flee.

It is a military stance where we grab hold of what the Word of God says about a matter and hammer satan with it. We are not those who back down; we are those who charge forward unafraid. This is our day to seize. I'm not suggesting we run into a situation without the solution of heaven first, but I am suggesting that when you have that solution, use it and do not let go of it until you see something break. Like a piece of pottery smashing on the ground, the places that have been long held in the enemy's grasp will shatter in a moment when you resist his ploys with forceful conviction. I am here to tell you today that you have the perseverance to continue, like the battering ram, to strike upon the promises of God for your life, your home, your family, and your nation. You have the perseverance that Jesus is speaking of here and you will be of those who will see the victory and release the prophetic solutions of heaven into the earth. The continual sacrifice of choosing to live in the place of seeing God's promises in the spirit before seeing them in the natural is what releases the iron scepter of your authority. Jesus is the battering ram of your authority, and it is He who smashes into pieces every trace of impossibility and rebellion in your life and in the earth.

"Is not My Word like fire," says the Lord, "and like iron that breaks a rock in pieces?" (Jeremiah 23:29 NLV)

STRIKE NOT ONCE OR TWICE

In case you're not familiar with the term *strike the ground* and where it came from, I want to further illustrate the picture of persistent prayer through this amazing story found in Second Kings 13:

Now Elisha had been suffering from the illness from which he died. Jehoash king of Israel went down to see him and

199

*wept over him. "My father! My father!" he cried. "The
chariots and horsemen of Israel!"*

*Elisha said, "Get a bow and some arrows," and he did so.
"Take the bow in your hands," he said to the king of Israel.
When he had taken it, Elisha put his hands on the king's
hands.*

*"Open the east window," he said, and he opened it. "Shoot!"
Elisha said, and he shot. "The Lord's arrow of victory, the
arrow of victory over Aram!" Elisha declared. "You will
completely destroy the Arameans at Aphek."*

*Then he said, "Take the arrows," and the king took them.
Elisha told him, "Strike the ground." He struck it three
times and stopped. The man of God was angry with him
and said, "You should have struck the ground five or six
times; then you would have defeated Aram and completely
destroyed it. But now you will defeat it only three times"*
(2 Kings 13:14-19 NIV).

I want to give you some context for Jeohash, the King of Israel in
this story. In verse 11 of this same chapter, the writer tells us that *"He
did evil in the eyes of the Lord and did not turn away from any of the sins
of Jeroboam son of Nebat, which he had caused Israel to commit; he continued in them"* (NIV). Why is this relevant? Well, first, Jeroboam was
accountable for introducing more idol worship in Israel, and it tells
us that Jehoash continued in that idol worship, among other things.
From this information alone, we know that Jehoash's heart was not
in a position of faith but rebellion when he came before Elisha. He
was overcome with fear and trembling because of the armies that
were coming up against him. I always wondered though—knowing

this, why did Elisha become angry with Jehoash when he didn't strike the ground more than three times? Elisha was never specific with him as to how many times he should have struck, so why was he angry? Then I realized—it is simply because Jehoash was not moving in faith. His heart was in a position of fear and it disabled the mission of prayer.

Verse 16 gives us further insight into the power of prophetic prayer: *"'Take the bow in your hands,' he said to the king of Israel. When he had taken it, Elisha put his hands on the king's hands"* (NIV). I love this verse. It's a beautiful picture of Jesus doing as Elisha did and placing His hands upon ours to strengthen us we strike in prayer. He adds His strength to our weakness. It's as though He is saying to you and me in this verse, "Hey, you're not alone. I'm with you. I'm holding you and steadying you, though you may feel scared or terrified at what is before you—just remember, it is by My strength and power that your victory comes. Simply trust Me." Don't be like Jehoash and partner with fear, but rather partner with faith and keep striking. When we continue to strike in prayer, like the battering ram, regardless of whether we see immediate change or not, we will see the victory.

BOLD FAITH

If faith is the substance of things hoped for, the evidence of things not seen, it is this kind of defiant faith that causes us to seize the promises we have been waiting for over our own lives, the lives of our families, our cities, and nations. Let me warn you, though, bold faith offends those who do not dare to believe. Bold faith interrupts their status quo and confronts their own beliefs of what they thought was acceptable. Bold faith attracts ridicule. But if you will continue, as the greats of our faith did, despite every opposition and mockery that may come your way, you will see the answer. Hebrews 11 is such an amazing chapter on this topic. I encourage you to read this chapter on your own, but for now, I want to pull on some of its most profound verses. It tells us:

> *Now faith brings our hopes into reality and becomes the foundation needed to acquire the things we long for. It is all the evidence required to prove what is still unseen. This testimony of faith is what previous generations were commended for. Faith empowers us to see that the universe was created and beautifully coordinated by the power of God's words! He spoke and the invisible realm gave birth to all that is seen* (Hebrews 11:1-3).

Prophetic prayer is no more than bold faith in action—by prophesying the answers and solutions of God's heart, we are bringing our hopes (and His) into reality.

Finally, again, this is reiterated in the following verses:

> *Through faith's power they conquered kingdoms and established true justice. Their faith fastened onto their promises and pulled them into reality! ...Faith sparked courage within them and they became mighty warriors in battle, pulling armies from another realm into battle array. Faith-filled women saw their dead children raised in resurrection power* (Hebrews 11:33-35).

I want you to truly allow those words to rest in your spirit.

"Through faith's power they conquered kingdoms and established true justice."
"Their faith fastened onto their promises and pulled them into reality!"
"They became mighty warriors in battle."
"Pulling armies from another realm into battle array."
"Faith-filled women saw their dead children raised in resurrection power."

Your persistence to stand in faith and release the prophetic decrees of heaven is far more powerful than you realize. Your faith is what conquers the kingdoms of this earth (the enemy); your faith is what pulls the promises and solutions of God into reality. Your faith is what releases the armies of heaven into battle array—they do the fighting, and you go down in the history books of eternity as a mighty warrior, all because you stood your ground. Faith raises the dead; faith interjects the natural realm and commands it to bow at the name of Jesus. Faith is a defiant act. But it is what brings heaven's promises into the earth.

PROPHETIC SOLUTION KEY #11

Pray with persistent faith.

What promises have you let go of that God is reminding you to pick up again and stand in defiant, bold, resilient faith with? Start striking the ground again. Remind yourself what God has spoken, what promises He has given you personally and governmentally—and begin waging war with your prophecies again.

NOTES

1. James W. Goll, *The Seer: Expanded Edition* (Shippensburg, PA: Destiny Image Publishers, 2012), 61.

2. "Battering ram," in Merriam-Webster's Dictionary, https://www .merriam-webster.com/dictionary/battering%20ram.

3. Battering ram except taken from our website: nateandchristy.co.

CHAPTER TWELVE

YOUR
COMMISSIONING

I'll never forget my earlier days of discovering and moving in prophetic prayer. One particular story has forever stayed with me. I had not long given birth to our first daughter and I was adjusting to the all-consuming world of having a newborn and being a stay-at-home mother. While I fully embraced and reveled in this new world of motherhood, I was also struggling with an uncomfortable agitation wrestling in my spirit. A war in my mind that told me my dreams and desires to see the kingdom of God established through my life were over and my life was now reduced to changing dirty diapers. I have to first reiterate—it was a dream come true becoming a new mother, but as with any dream fulfilled, the enemy has a tendency of attempting to belittle the season you are in to rob you of strength and joy in the process. The Holy Spirit, however, had a different plan. He was about to show me something very powerful by revealing to me that my desire to raise a family and my desire to see His kingdom established through my life were one and the same. He was about to show me how the two could work together, and how I could do it right where I was, without having to leave my living room while in this season of my life. I believe this is a common weapon of the enemy—to attempt to convince you and me that the current seasons of our lives are unimportant. He then attempts to persuade us into inactivity by making us believe that God cannot use us right where we are at. These are his frivolous pursuits to block prophetic prayer.

The Holy Spirit showed me through this one experience just how deceitful those thoughts are. One afternoon while Nate was at work, I was nursing our newborn daughter and watching a midday movie on television. During the commercials, a news report appeared about a missing child. This missing boy had been a high-profile case in our nation of Australia for well over eight years by that point. The news was reporting that his parents were growing weary in their search. Every small piece of evidence had led investigators to dead ends and the reporter was sharing how they were growing more and more desperate to find him. A wave of emotion overtook me, and I began to weep as I looked down at my own child, struggling to comprehend the pain that his parents must have been feeling.

Looking back on this moment, I recognize what was happening. It was the gift of prophetic prayer, though I didn't understand it at the time. The Holy Spirit had arrested my emotions and rose up within me to cry out on behalf of these parents for justice. Something inside of me began stirring, a bubbling sense of fiery justice that grew stronger with each second that passed. I had felt it only a handful of times before—this feeling of a volcano erupting within me as His Spirit burst out of me. With tears streaming down my face, the bubbling was now raging like a furious fire of righteous anger for these parents. I began shouting into heaven, jolting my poor sleeping newborn awake. I clearly remember these words bursting out of my mouth: "Father God, *release* angels right now to reveal the blueprints of where this child is, whether he is dead or alive. Your Word says in Mark 4:22 that you will uncover everything that has been hidden and you will bring it into the light. I decree *justice* for this boy, I decree justice for his family, I decree Your answers to be released on their behalf. Father, reveal where he is and bring closure for this family."

LEGISLATING GOD'S ORIGINAL DESIGN

Prophetic prayer is the combined gift of intercession and prophecy. Though you may not feel called to the office of intercession, I believe God has equipped each and every son and daughter with a portion of this gift. The partnership of prophecy and intercession is a powerful force when wielded together. It legislates heaven to earth, and you have been given this gift, whether male or female, to release His heart into every problem. There is a common misconception that prayer and intercession is mainly for women, but I believe that God is raising up a company of both sons and daughters who will effectively release the strategies of heaven into the earth in our present day and age.

We've touched a lot on what prophecy is throughout this book—how it is the spoken answers of God's heart over a situation and the release of His solutions ahead of time. But what role does intercession play? Isn't intercession just prayer? I want to show you through the Greek and Hebrew definitions of this word how intercession is not some untouchable and overwhelming gift that is reserved for a special few. Prophecy and prayer combined is, in fact, intercession.

Let's take a quick look at the Greek and Hebrew meanings of the word *intercession* and piece the last puzzle piece together of just how powerful this weapon of prophetic prayer actually is. The Greek word for intercession is *huperentugchanó* or *hyperentygxánō* (Strong's, G5241, 5228). Combined, these two words mean "to make petition for." *Huperentugchanó* is a compound word; when we break it down the two words within it read *huper*, meaning "for benefit," and *entygxánō*, meaning "to come in line with." It is also defined as a bending over to confer benefit. The Hebrew word for intercession is *paga`* and it means "to meet, encounter, reach, and to attack violently." How does this apply to you in prophetic prayer and praying the promises of heaven? When you are praying on behalf of another, you are in fact bending down to their need and conferring the benefit of the cross and releasing the resurrection life of Jesus to reach and encounter them. It is a fierce act of prayer that commands the impossibilities to shift, causing the Spirit of God to be released into a situation and encounter it with His solutions. It is a petition on behalf of another by calling a violation back into alignment according to the Word of God. Many have side-stepped away from intercession for misunderstanding of this gift, but I believe God is bringing the body of Christ into a full revelation of what our prayers and intercessions can and will do.

You may remember our discussion about authoring with Christ—how we are called to bring that which is out of order back into His perfect alignment. This is your commissioning of prophetic prayer. Praying the promises of heaven over your home family and nation is in its simplest form calling that which is in violation and rewriting it with the Blood of the Lamb back into innocence again, as Paul writes in Colossians so beautifully:

> *For through the Son everything was created, both in the heavenly realm and on the earth, all that is seen and all that is unseen. Every seat of power, realm of government, principality, and authority—it was all created through him and for his purpose! He existed before anything was made, and now everything finds completion in him* (Colossians 1:16-17).
>
> *For God is satisfied to have all his fullness dwelling in Christ. And by the blood of his cross, everything in heaven and earth is brought back to himself—**back to its original intent, restored to innocence again!*** (Colossians 1:19-20)

This is your assignment—to use the weapon of prophetic prayer to call that which is out of alignment and bring it back into its original intent, restored to innocence again. If a loved one is living a life of sin and is lost, you have the power and authority in Christ to use prophetic prayer as your weapon to call them back into completion in Jesus. By His Blood that continues to speak and work to this day, we call anything that is in disarray and out of order, and we command it to come back into His fullness again.

RESTORING TO INNOCENCE

When I prayed that impassioned plea on behalf of the family whose son was missing, I had no idea that I had just released a decree of heaven to earth in prophetic prayer and, like arrows released from my mouth, the result of that one decree caused an immediate turn of events. As anyone who has a newborn may remember, you very quickly forget things and get lost in time. So, when the next day came and I was sitting back down for my newly established routine of nursing and a midday movie, I was not expecting what was about to happen. A breaking news report interrupted the movie with the scrolling title down the bottom of the screen, which read: "(Boy's name) whereabouts breakthrough!" My jaw dropped as the reality of my prayer from the day before hit me hard. I was honestly stunned. I did not expect such an immediate response to my prayer from the day before, and I had since forgotten all about it. The news reporter repeated these words over and over, "This is unprecedented!" They went on to reveal that in the afternoon on the day before, which would have been immediately after I had prayed, they received an anonymous tip for a lead on the whereabouts of the missing boy. This tip immediately led investigators to a man and within days it was revealed that he had in fact murdered this young child. While it was devastating to hear what had happened to the boy, this information led his parents to his precise resting location, and they were able to retrieve the remains of his body and give him the burial he deserved. His parents were able to receive closure, and within two months after that prayer the man who had murdered him was convicted of murder after eight long years of no leads or answers.

While I know it was not my prayers alone that brought about this answer, I know that God allowed me to be a part of it. He wanted to teach me that my hands were not tied, and I could change the world right where I was, changing diapers and all. He wanted to show me

His desires to uncover hidden secrets and bring answers into the light. I fervently believe it is the desire of God for every one of His sons and daughters to operate in the full authority that has been given to us to establish His kingdom upon the earth. What does that look like? I believe it is the release of solutions, answers, and strategies for every problem. I believe it is His glory made manifest in such a way that people encounter God right where they are—driving to work, sitting in their offices, or at home with their children. When the sons and daughters of the King show up, He shows up too, and it affects all realms of society. Can you imagine sitting in your car waiting at the traffic lights, immersed in the continual presence of God, and then looking to your left and noticing the person next to you crying because they suddenly feel His presence too? What if this is what the kingdom of God was meant to look like? An explosive force of His undeniable presence released into every sphere of the earth. I believe this is just the beginning, and it is you and I who carry the answers to these impossibilities.

God longs to reveal Himself through these answers by delivering people out of their bondage. All too often, however, we believe the lie that our current season needs to be different, or we need more finances, or that God can't use us right where we are at. If you have picked up this book, I can say with confidence that I know you already have an appetite for the impossible. How can I possibly know that? Because every person on earth has been embedded with that desire because we were each made in the image of our Father, the God of the impossible. Yet it is only through intimate relationship with Jesus where this supernatural ability is activated. The enemy will try and convince you that you are not ready, that you are not qualified; I am here to tell you that you are. I am here to tell you that it is time for His glory to shine upon you, His answers to be seen within you, and His kingdom to be released through you. It is your time to rise in the fullness of the authority Jesus died for you to have.

THE CALL TO SUBJUGATE

God's commissioning to Adam and Eve in Genesis 1:28 has been re-given to you and me: *"God blessed them and said to them, 'Be fruitful and increase in number; fill the earth and subdue it'"* (NIV). The word for *subdue* in Hebrew is an interesting one. It is the word *kabash*, and it literally means "to force into bondage, bring into subjection, subjugate, and tread under foot" (Strong's, H3533). That could sound like an oppressive command if you didn't know who Adam and Eve were commissioned to subdue. The only other inhabitants of the earth at that time were God, Adam and Eve, the animals, and the enemy. God had given Adam and Eve a commissioning to rule and reign over satan and his demon cohorts, to bring them into subjection and tread upon them with their feet. We know that Adam and Eve were unable to fulfill that command, but Jesus did. One of my favorite verses in Colossians describes that sweet moment of victory when Jesus triumphed for us:

> *Then Jesus made a public spectacle of all the powers and principalities of darkness, stripping away from them every weapon and all their spiritual authority and power to accuse us. And by the power of the cross, Jesus led them*

around as prisoners in a procession of triumph. He was not their prisoner; they were his! (Colossians 2:15)

Do you see that all power and authority was stripped from the enemy, given into your hands, and commissioned to you with the full backing of the Blood of Jesus behind you? This means that every time you wield the weapon of the Word of God by His Blood, you will have victory. In some cases, you will see immediate results; in other cases, you may need to stand in the fight a while longer, but you can be guaranteed of this one thing—victory is yours, every single time, if you simply don't give up.

OVERCOMER OF THE AGES

In the beginning processes of piecing together this book for you, the Holy Spirit led me to a profound revelation written within Paul's first letter to the Corinthians. This portion of his letter that I will share with you in a moment is the revelation that I have built every chapter within this book upon. Before I share his words with you, I want to first highlight the audience to which Paul was writing. Corinth was known to be one of the Roman Empire's most powerful, rich, and yet promiscuous cities. It was well known throughout the provinces as a den of iniquity and idolatry, and people would travel from all over the world to come and taste of all it had to offer. Ancient Corinth was also known for its worldly orators and philosophers. There are historical reports of "the seven wise men of Greece" whose literature and quotes were revered throughout the provinces of the Roman and Greek empires. One such quote from one of the seven wise men that shaped the way Greeks and Romans alike perceived the world was "You should never desire the impossible" by Chilon of Sparta. When you consider this kind of worldly wisdom that the city of Corinth revered, you can understand with deeper gratitude what it was Paul was writing to the church there. Within this difficult climate, Paul planted the congregation of Corinth, and to this day his letters to them are some of our most cherished in the New Testament. The Corinthian church was given the task of being light in the darkness, starkly opposing the philosophies, idolatry, and iniquity by staunchly adhering to the words of Jesus and Paul's instructions.

When you consider the cultural climate of Corinth, it is easy see that it mirrors our own current cultural climate. The world has become infatuated with worldly wisdom; they have embraced idolatry and normalized iniquity. In many ways, we are the modern-day Corinthian church which Paul was writing to. In light of this, I want you to read his words and consider the depths of what he is charging you and me to walk in. He writes:

> *However, there is a wisdom that we continually speak of when we are among the spiritually mature. It's wisdom that didn't originate in this present age, nor did it come from the rulers of this age who are in the process of being dethroned. Instead, we continually speak of this wonderful wisdom that comes from God, hidden before now in a mystery. It is his secret plan, destined before the ages, to bring us into glory. None of the rulers of this present world order understood it, for if they had, they never would have*

crucified the Lord of shining glory. This is why ι
tures say:

> *Things never discovered or heard of before,*
> *things beyond our ability to imagine—these are the*
> *many things God has in store*
> *for all his lovers.*

But God now unveils these profound realities to us by
the Spirit. Yes, he has revealed to us his inmost heart and
deepest mysteries through the Holy Spirit, who constantly
explores all things. After all, who can really see into a per-
son's heart and know his hidden impulses except for that
person's spirit? So it is with God. His thoughts and secrets
are only fully understood by his Spirit, the Spirit of God.

For we did not receive the spirit of this world system but
the Spirit of God, so that we might come to understand
and experience all that grace has lavished upon us. And
we articulate these realities with the words imparted to
us by the Spirit and not with the words taught by human
wisdom. We join together Spirit-revealed truths with Spir-
it-revealed words. Someone living on an entirely human
level rejects the revelations of God's Spirit, for they make
no sense to him. He can't understand the revelations of the
Spirit because they are only discovered by the illumination
of the Spirit. Those who live in the Spirit are able to care-
fully evaluate all things, and they are subject to the scrutiny
of no one but God. For

Who has ever intimately known the mind of the Lord Yahweh well enough to become his counselor?

Christ has, and we possess Christ's perceptions (1 Corinthians 2:6-16).

This is such a powerful declaration over us. We hold the keys of godly wisdom that the earth is so desperately searching for and unable to find. It is not the inferior wisdom of this world, but the superior wisdom of our King. We have been given a gift, found within His wisdom, to release the answers and solutions of His heart that will dethrone the wisdom of this age and ultimately bring the lost home. Notice it says we *articulate.* There is action involved. We evaluate and discern through our "organ of sense," we discern the higher ways and thoughts of God by His Spirit, for we possess Christ's perceptions and then we articulate those perceptions through our decrees. I also find it so incredible that Paul writes about the ages within these verses—that Jesus *is* the overcomer of the ages. That just as the worldly wisdom of Corinth eventually crumbled into nothingness, Christ's wisdom still stands. We will see the wisdom, idolatries, and violations of our present age crumble and fall before us as we release His Spirit into everything that is out of order. His wisdom outlasts the ages and we have the supernatural ability to wield His wisdom as a weapon, to destroy and dethrone every demonic power and principality. I believe we are entering a time when the world leaders and kings of this earth will search you out. They will hunger after the superior wisdom of God that you carry. They will ask you to help them uncover mysteries, just as Daniel was gifted to do.

I want you to read the last verse from the paragraph of Paul's letter, and I ask you to pause upon it. Really consider what it is that God is saying to you right now:

> *For who has ever intimately known the mind of the Lord Yahweh well enough to become his counselor? Christ has, and we possess Christ's perceptions* (1 Corinthians 2:16).

YOU POSSESS CHRIST'S PERCEPTIONS

God is lifting the veil in this day and hour when His sons and daughters are about to discover things beyond what we ever could have imagined and they will be revealed by His Spirit. He longs to reveal to you the secrets of His inmost heart, the solutions and strategies of heaven, and the mysteries that are hidden from this world. We are of a higher system; when we come into His presence, we are lifted above this world system and we receive and release His higher realities into the earth around us.

Jesus has overcome the ages. We are not stuck in this age of apparent confusion and distraction, but it is in the process of being dethroned as we move into position in the secret place, perceive what He is saying because we possess what He perceives, and we then articulate and release His desires. Your commissioning of prophetic prayer is to release the victorious name of Jesus into the earth as it says, *"But thanks be to God! He gives us the victory through our Lord Jesus Christ"* (1 Cor. 15:57 NIV), and, *"No, in all these things we are more than conquerors through him who loved us"* (Rom. 8:37 NIV).

These verses are a promise to us that every time we see a problem, whether a personal problem, a family crisis, or a dilemma in the earth, we can look at that situation square in the eye and remind it that it must bow to the victorious name of Jesus. His name is the solution. His name is the reason that we are here. Romans 11:36 tells us that *"from him and through him and for him are all things. To him be the glory forever! Amen"* (NIV). When something is not aligning with His perfect will, you can author it to return to its original design in Jesus.

AUTHORING HEAVEN

When the Holy Spirit first gave me the concepts of this book, He gave me a picture of a mother who was cooking her family dinner. She had a baby in one arm, but He showed me what she was holding in the spirit—she had a sword in the other hand. As she was cooking dinner while holding her baby, she was also waging war in the heavenly realms. She was worshiping and singing and there was a sense of joy and purpose that surrounded her. As a result, her family was happy, her children were running around laughing, and she too was laughing in joy. She was in two places at once—serving her family and taking ground in the spirit as she released prophetic prayer from her kitchen table.

Maybe you are that mother with a baby in your arms (this is not a stereotype of mothers at home, simply to share what I saw in my spirit). Or maybe you are the husband cooking your family a meal and praying with the sword in the other hand. Perhaps you are a magnate in the business world, or you are a freshman in college, or you are working around the clock in a start-up business. Maybe you're a grandparent or a teacher in a classroom. Whatever your position, the purpose behind this book is for every son and daughter to recognize the weapon that is already in your hands. A weapon so powerful that it will turn the tide of the impossibilities that dare to surround you. All it takes is for you to lean on the chest of the Father, listen for His voice, and then prophesy the solutions He reveals to you with His name as your weapon. My hope and prayer for you is that this authority within you awakens, because it is the desire of God for you to move mountains with Him from wherever it is that you occupy.

You do not need a bachelor's degree or a Bible school degree to answer the Father's call in praying prophetic prayers and releasing His solutions. While education and degrees are great, they are not the qualifying factors that the Father looks for. He looks for a heart that is for Him and hungry to see impossibilities turn. If that resonates with you, then you are ready. You can still go to Bible school and get the bachelor's degree, but you don't need to wait until then. If God can use a fifteen-year-old boy to take down a giant of impossibility, He can use you right where you are. Whether you are changing diapers or overseeing corporations, you are positioned through the power of your prophetic prayers to release the solutions of God into the earth.

What could the earth look like if we intentionally grasped this revelation with everything that we have? What if we saw every injustice and every violation as an opportunity to release God's heart? What if we didn't wait for the next person to answer that problem, but we took responsibility and went directly to the heart of the Father and asked Him what He desires to do to invade that darkness? What if we looked at the earth not as something that we need to escape from but as a gift that God has given to us to restore through the precious Blood of Jesus? His Blood isn't only for our redemption, though in itself our salvation is profoundly powerful. His Blood is also the ongoing power to redeem everything around us. Far too many see the Blood of Jesus as just a one-way ticket to heaven, and while that standing alone is far too great to comprehend, the Blood of Jesus is so much more. It is the power to rewrite every wrong, it is the authority to redeem the entire earth, it is the transformative power to supernaturally replant the Garden of Eden into the earth. Imagine what God's original design of delight could look like if it covered the earth? Is it possible? I wholeheartedly believe it is. Mass revivals broke out from small pockets of gatherings such as Azusa Street, a revival so transformative that it completely changed the face of Christianity to this day. You and I wouldn't be reading books such as this one if it was not for that small group of believers who faithfully gathered to pray in a run-down part of Los Angeles. Imagine what a company of believers who wholeheartedly carry this mandate could do. Imagine if we simply believed. Imagine if we got bold enough to step outside of our comfort zones to give ourselves to this very thing? Imagine if we gave our lives for the laid-down purpose of releasing the kingdom of God into the earth.

The earth can indeed look like heaven, just as the prophets foretold. Your life has been marked by God from the beginning of the ages for this very thing. The purpose you seek is found in seeking

Him and releasing His glory into the earth. I want to finish with this scripture from Colossians:

> *Your hearts can soar with joyful gratitude when you think of how God made you worthy to receive the glorious inheritance freely given to us by living in the light. He has rescued us* **completely** *from the tyrannical rule of darkness and has translated us into the kingdom realm of His beloved Son. For in the Son* **all** *our sins are canceled and we have the* **release** *of* **redemption through his very blood** (Colossians 1:12-13).

What more can be said? His Blood *releases* redemption to us, and we have the privilege of releasing His redemption to the world around us. I don't know about you, but I don't want to get to heaven and realize that I wasted the one fleeting chance I had on this earth and averted my God-given authority for a life less than what His Blood paid for. I want to know that my time was spent on Him. I want to know that I gave myself for Him. I want to know that the cause of my obedience sent ripple waves of supernatural effect into eternity. How about you? You are not here reading these words by accident; the Holy Spirit has led you here for there is a stirring growing deep within you, a holy agitation for more, a bubbling of His Spirit that is beckoning you to reach out and step out beyond what you thought were limitations and launch into the unknown with Him. He is calling—will you respond? You carry the solution of heaven, Jesus Christ, within you. It's time to release Him into everything that stands in opposition to His original design. Are you ready? It's your time.

PROPHETIC SOLUTION KEY #12

Pray the Blood of Jesus.

You have been commissioned to a lifestyle of aligning the earth with what the Blood of Jesus purchased. The Blood of Jesus is more than a key; it's the doorway to daily victorious prayer wherever you choose to release it. Where has God called you? What is your mission field? It's time for you to write and rewrite history with your prophetic prayers and decrees!

ABOUT CHRISTY JOHNSTON

CHRISTY JOHNSTON is an intercessor, teacher, prophetic voice, and justice carrier. Christy's burning heart for justice and intercession has led her on a life journey of prayer, contending for major world issues. Together with her husband, Nate, and their two young daughters, she is passionate to raise and empower God's sons and daughters to release the kingdom of God across the earth.

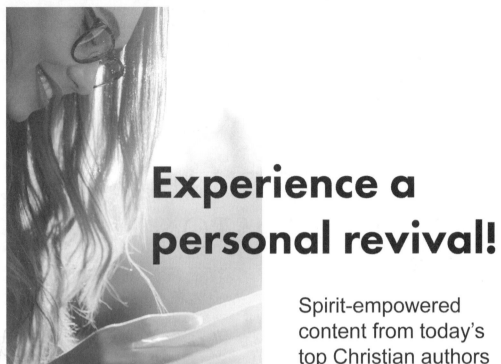